FALSE LOVE ALWAYS GIVES SIGHT

F.L.A.G.S.

By

Harnetha Shantrā

Published By
Visions In Motion Productions
ISBN-13: 978-0692661956
ISBN-10: 0692661956

DEDICATION

To everyone *looking to give and receive true love that will last for a lifetime.*

ACKNOWLEDGEMENTS

I give thanks to God and His son, Jesus. I'm blessed to have a wonderful, and supportive mother, Peggy C. McCoy, for raising me into a God fearing woman. I'm thankful for my late grandparents, Robert & Lillie Mae McCoy, for building a great foundation for our family to stand on. To Johnny Lee Holman Jr., thank you for allowing me to feel the love of a man.

To my church family for life, Christ Abundant Life Christian Ministries and Apostle Derrick E. Flanagan Sr. & Pastor Charmaine Flanagan, please know I love you dearly. You have instilled great values in me and, because of you, I will forever know who I AM.

To the many false loves I've encountered, I'm still standing. To William *Jeremy* Almon - my brother, my angel, gone too soon - thank you for watching over me. And lastly, my best, and most important, Ryan, Jessica, and Naomi I love you with all my heart, it was because of you "I survived". When failed relationships had me feeling like throwing in the towel on life, it was your beautiful faces and smiles God brought before me that pulled me through. ~my3nme~

CONTENTS

←CHAPTER ONE→
Turning Point

When two people meet, they are auditioning for roles in each other's lives. The question you have to ask yourself is. What role does this person want to play in my life?

It was a warm fall evening in Atlanta, Ga. as Reagan drove the long stretch of I-20 westbound to her mother's home. She was devastated because the reality of yet another failed relationship was once again right before her.

Reagan found it more and more difficult to drive because her eyes were filled with tears. *How did I get to this place again? Will anyone ever truly love me?* Reagan filled the car with a loud scream.

There were people in Reagan's circle who believed that her being gay was due to some generational curses from her past. Reagan's mother got saved when she was nine years old. From that point on they never missed a church service. Reagan's mom took Reagan and her brother Maurice to two services on Sunday; Wednesday and Friday night Bible Study; prayer meetings; and various rehearsals. According to her mom, there was never an excuse good enough to miss church.

Reagan was raised to believe that the gay lifestyle was an abomination to God and all gay people would burn in hell for an eternity. So whenever she went through breakups with her lesbian lovers, her mind couldn't help but to wonder if through the prayers of her family and loved ones, was God was punishing her and would never allow her to be happy with a woman.

Reagan's mind started to drift back to her childhood, around the age of six when her mother would leave her at a friend's house while she went out clubbing (before she got saved, of course). Reagan would cling and hold on to her mom because she didn't want her to leave her there. Reagan's mom was around 24 years old and a party girl who couldn't wait to hit the streets on the weekend.

Reagan's grandparents would keep her and her brother Maurice for the most part, but every now and then would tell her mom no in an effort to make her more responsible. Whenever they told her no she would find friends to leave them with, which meant separating them from time to time.

Reagan didn't want her mom to leave because she knew what was going to happen to her after she was gone. Reagan could see him sitting in front of the TV in his recliner chair, chain smoking his cigarettes and drinking liquor. His eyes were fixed on her. She could feel an empty hole in the pit of her stomach.

Reagan was very scared because she knew what was going to happen after everybody went to bed.

After she got older, Reagan understood why her mom chose to leave her there. Her best friend had a daughter Madison, who was Reagan's age, and she and Reagan played very well together. Madison would come to Reagan's house to play sometimes. Reagan always cried and pleaded with her mom not to leave her at Madison's house. If only she had the courage to tell her mom what was happening to her in that home. After a few hours of playing with Madison's large dollhouse, it would get late and Madison's grandmother would announce it was time to get ready for bed.

Once in bed, Reagan always tried to keep her friend Madison awake as long as she could. Because she knew he was coming in the room once he thought everyone was sleeping. For hours Madison and Reagan would talk and giggle about everything, mostly boys, since they went to different schools. Yes, boys; Reagan didn't always dislike boys or, should we say, maybe she wasn't "born" this way.

But if you asked Reagan today, she would say she believes sexual preference is something you are born with, and that some develop their true feelings quicker than others. In her early years she always felt uncomfortable around girls; they made her feel very nervous. Reagan was much more comfortable around boys. Since she didn't quite understand what was going on with her feelings, it took her longer than others to realize her attraction for women.

After losing the battle of keeping her host for the evening awake, Reagan found herself lying in the dark room too afraid to let herself fall asleep.

She could see into Madison's large walk-in closet and was amazed at all the pretty dresses and shoes Madison had in there; they were all hers and she didn't even have to share with anybody. She was an only child. Reagan wore a lot of hand me downs from her cousin.

15

Madison's parents were not married but her dad took really good care of her financially.

Reagan clinched the blanket tight around her body as she heard his footsteps coming down the long hallway. The door slowly opened; she could smell the cigar and hear him breathing as he stood in the doorway watching her. There were twin beds in the room and he walked over to the bed Reagan was lying on. His cold, fat, and rough hands fumbled around in the blanket and grabbed Reagan's arm, pulling her closer to him. He flipped her over on her back, and pulled her pajama pants and panties off. He was breathing heavy in her face with the smell of stale cigarettes and liquor on his breath. Reagan's eyes filled with tears, her heart pounding.

"No, Pleeeeease," Reagan cried softly, remembering what he would do if she cried too loud.

"Shut up!" he said, pinching her nose with force. Reagan lay there with tears streaming down her face.

She thought about her mom and hated her at that moment for what she was going through. He proceeded to climb on top of her and begin roughly foundling her with his fat fingers. He then forced himself inside of her, having his way. It was very painful for Reagan, she felt hatred for him and often thought about taking his life. She felt like she was worthless, that nobody cared for her or loved her. She thought about her dad and wondered why he wasn't in her life.

Where is my daddy? She thought. Would he beat this man up for doing this to his little girl? Reagan wondered.

He growled and released himself inside of her tiny frail body. He rolled off her and left the room.

This abuse went on until Reagan's mother got saved but Reagan never told anyone because of the fear she had for this man and the threats he made to her that he would kill her mom and her brother Maurice. It took a lot of time and healing to get over these acts of molestation, physical, and mental abuse. Reagan at such a young age had to endure a lot of pain both physically and emotionally. And she had to do it alone.

As years passed by she became a rebellious pre-teen, getting into trouble in school for fighting, skipping classes and being extremely disrespectful to teachers. Her mother had grown up around this family and had no idea he committed these acts against her daughter. Years later, they learned he was arrested and prosecuted for molesting Reagan's little playmate, his own niece Madison. Reagan always wondered if it was happening to Madison too, but never had the courage to talk to her about it. Reagan had resentment in her heart towards her parents; she blamed them for what happened to her. She blamed her mother for leaving her there in the first place, and her father for not being in her life.

Out of the twenty-two grandchildren her grandparents had, Reagan was the only one who had no father in her life. If you looked up the word deadbeat in the dictionary there would be a picture of Reagan's dad there as the prime example. It was tough for Reagan to see her cousins spend time with their dads. She was happy for them but it reminded her of the absence of her own dad and sent the message to her that he didn't love and care enough for her to be there, to protect her. How could Reagan know her worth if her own father rejected her?

Did being molested by a trusted friend of the family, the sometimes neglect from her mother, or rejection from her father cause Reagan to become a lesbian? Some might draw that conclusion, although there are straight women who went through sexual violations as children as well. Reagan believed that sexual preference is based on your own will and desire deep within you. We as individuals choose or suppress whom we love. Those who choose to suppress their feelings usually end up living an "in the closet" lifestyle.

Reagan had an attraction to boys until she was eleven years old. After that, she started developing and understanding her feelings for girls. By this time, her mother was well into the Pentecostal Church so she had no choice but to suppress her homosexual feelings.

She was being taught, and during that time believed that the God who made her would burn her in a lake of fire for eternity. Therefore, she wouldn't dare let anybody know what she was feeling inside.

←CHAPTER TWO→
Foundations

God has spared my life for the second time, Reagan thought to herself. "This woman really could have killed me," Reagan thought, and then burst into an uncontrollable cry. Her mom walked over to her and began rubbing her on the back in efforts to comfort her.

"Oh baby, God has the right one for you," her soft voice said.

"But it hurts so bad," Reagan cried. "Will someone ever love me?

"I'm such a good person to everybody I deal with. Why do they take my kindness as a weakness?" Reagan cried.

"Just pray and ask God. He will direct you, her mom replied. "Remember, and this too shall pass."

That night, Reagan prayed and even thanked God for delivering her from the mentally abusive, near deadly situation she had just come from with Don. The life had literally been sucked right out of her and, at that moment, she knew it was up to her and only her to turn things around.

Reagan was raised approximately 35 minutes west of Atlanta, Georgia in a small town called Winston. Her family didn't have much money at all. She was her mother's second child but her mother never married either one of their fathers.

They lived with her grandparents, who did what they could to help her mom out. Reagan's grandparents didn't have much money, either. They lived in a small three-bedroom home, thirteen people in all. There was plenty of love and food so they were quite happy.

Reagan's mother had a lot of male friends and she enjoyed entertaining them. She spent most weekends were spent with her friends, leaving Reagan with her grandparents. Reagan would lie in bed crying until she fell asleep. She longed for her mother's attention most of her childhood. Reagan's grandfather was the only father figure she had, but he spent most of his time working or sitting outside alone smoking his Camel cigarettes. Sometimes Reagan would go sit in the yard with him for hours just to talk. Though she always knew her grandfather loved her, he wasn't the affectionate type so he never said it. In fact, Reagan was never told "I love you" by a male figure at any point in her childhood.

Reagan's grandparents had eight children and four of them - including Reagan's mom - still lived at home, along with their children. There were seven kids in the house so they had to share everything. The thing Reagan hated sharing more than anything was her big brother

Maurice. She felt hurt because she never could seem to win his attention over that of her cousins. Reagan and Maurice had different fathers but Maurice was related to the other cousins in the house on both their mom and dad's side of the family. Maurice and the other cousins would tease Reagan by saying they were double cousins. It made Reagan feel like her brother didn't value their relationship. To this day, Reagan feels as if her brother is ashamed of her, because of her lesbian lifestyle.

Reagan always told her friends that if her father walked into a room she was in that she wouldn't know who he was because he never made an effort to get into her life. Reagan's dad called her on the phone once when she was nine years old. She was so nervous talking to him and it was so overwhelming for her that she burst into tears as soon as they hung up. It was Christmas season and he had asked her what she wanted for Christmas that year. With excitement, she told him all about this dollhouse she wanted. Reagan knew her mom couldn't afford it so deep down, she really wanted to believe he would buy it for her. Not only did he not buy the dollhouse, Reagan never heard from him again.

Some people would say Reagan is a lesbian because she felt rejected and abused by all the men in her life but it is unfair to judge how people deal with their life struggles. Reagan looked at it this way: there are far more straight men and women out there who were abused, neglected, and raised with one parent in their homes, as well as homosexuals out there who were raised with both parents in the home and faced no abuse whatsoever.

Reagan could be her whole, true self with women. She felt normal and natural even though everybody around her said it was unnatural. Being with women made Reagan want more; she had this instant drive to make things better for her and her mate.

What she found with men, in terms of dealing with a woman's tomboyish ways, is they would always want to come to her house and watch movies and order take-out. She felt like they didn't want to be seen out with her.

She would sometimes get this vibe from other women: if they were interested in feminine women only or with women on the down low, they appeared to want people to see them as just two friends hanging out.

In the black lesbian community women mostly refer to themselves as Studs and Fems. A Stud usually dresses like a dude and wears her haircut like one or dreads. Some will even wear men's underwear. Most Studs are the dominant ones in a relationship so a Stud will rarely date another Stud.

Fems usually dress very feminine, wear heels, keep their hair and nails done, and are generally submissive. Most Fems will date another fem, but there are some Fems who will not date a Stud because of her personal preference. For example, some Fems will say "I like women, so I want my woman to look like a woman." Or maybe she's not "out of the closet" and don't want the attention when she's on a date with her mate.

Reagan disliked labels, although most people viewed her as a Stud, which she absolutely hated. She loved sports, hates wearing heels, wears her hair short, hates dresses, and loves to put on a pair of Jordan's. When people asked her if she' was a Stud or Fem her answer was always "I'm Reagan." It bothered Reagan that there is self-discrimination within the lesbian community.

Reagan felt that if two Studs fall in love with each other and wanted to date, people shouldn't give them a hard time about it. To Reagan, it was no different from any other discrimination in the world. After all love is love, right?

←CHAPTER THREE→
The Encounter

Reagan's first intimate encounter with a woman is a day she will never forget. It was a strong and passionate sexual encounter with an older female teenager. Sidney was the older sister of Reagan's best friend Brea. She was seventeen - three years older than Reagan - and the captain of the local high school varsity basketball team.

Sidney was very popular, beautiful and loved sports. She had long, soft silky hair, the kind that black people would call "good hair," which she always wore pulled back in a ponytail. She was a little taller than Reagan, who was tall for her age. She was what we called a red bone and had light brown eyes. Sidney had an athletic build, six-pack and all.

Sidney and Brea's parents were very liberal and knew of her sexuality. They raised their girls to feel free to express themselves. Sidney came out to them at a young age: When she was four years old, she asked her mom if she could take a little girl in her pre-k class some chocolates for Valentine Day. Her mom sat her down and had a talk with her to confirm her suspicions.

Reagan caught herself staring at Sidney a lot, fantasizing about her all the time. She noticed how nice Sidney was to her whenever she visited their home. Reagan's favorite candy bar was Snickers and Sidney seemed to always have one for her.

Sidney would routinely choose Reagan to be on her team for outside neighborhood games and would partner up with her for board games. Reagan loved and needed the attention she received from Sidney, who made her feel special. No one ever made her feel this way before. Reagan certainly didn't understand the feelings because, at the age of fourteen and being raised with Christian beliefs, she just couldn't wrap her head around where these wrong feelings she had come from. What did she do to make her this bad person her church family spoke of? She decided to brush it off, and figured she and Sidney was just more compatible as friends than she and Brea. Until it happened...

One Saturday, Reagan was supposed to meet her best friend Brea at her house to work on a school project. Reagan walked up to the door and rang the doorbell. Sidney came to the door and informed Reagan that her sister wasn't home, that she was running errands with their mom.

"Come on in, they'll be back shortly," Sidney said.

Reagan had mixed feelings about coming inside and being alone with Sidney, because she didn't trust her own feelings towards Sidney. Reagan reluctantly followed

Sidney inside, but deep down she wanted nothing more than to be alone with Sidney.

Sidney was wearing a navy blue sports bra, white wife beater, baby blue basketball shorts, white ankle socks, and a pair of Nike flip-flops. Her body was perfectly formed. Reagan caught a nice whiff of Sidney as she passed by her to come inside the house and she smelled so good.

"You can come to my room, I was just playing a video game," she said.

Reagan followed her down the long hallway to Sidney's room. She sat on the foot of the bed. Sidney handed her a controller. "Here, let's play," she said.

As Reagan grabbed the controller, Sidney's hand gently brushed across hers and their eyes met. Sidney quickly turned her head to the TV.

"Okay, let's go," she said.

31

The girls were teamed up, running from and fighting aliens while trying to get back to the safe house. Thanks to Maurice, Reagan was actually pretty good at the game and they made it to the safe house. They threw up their controllers, screamed with joy, gave each other a high five, and started jumping up and down.

"You're really good," she said. "You play much?"

"Yeah, with my brother, Reagan said.

Somehow, the girls fell onto the bed with Sidney landing on top of Reagan, looking down into her eyes. Reagan gazed back into Sidney's beautiful eyes.

"Can I kiss you?" Sidney asked.

"Sure," Reagan whispered. With her body filled with nervousness that was all she could utter.

Sidney softly licked her lips and planted a nice, soft kiss on Reagan's lips. Sidney pulled back, kissing her several more times. She came in for another kiss and this time was different - she slid her tongue into Reagan's mouth and began to softly but passionately kiss her as she rubbed her hand up and down Reagan's stomach and inner thighs.

Reagan began to feel something within her come alive and it felt so good. She couldn't control her breathing; she couldn't tell which was louder - her breathing or her heartbeat. Sidney kept asking Reagan if she was okay and if she wanted her to stop but stopping was the last thing Reagan wanted her to do. As her tongue went deeper, and deeper in Reagan's mouth, the wetter her panties got. Sidney slid her hand down Reagan's pants, and into her panties.

"Oh, my gosh. You are so fucking wet!" Sidney said.

She rubbed the tips of her fingers in a circular motion around Reagan's private area, making sure to gently stroke her clit. This made Reagan explode and she began to moan louder and louder with passion.

Sidney started sucking on her younger lover's neck and chest area, whispering in her ear how good she tasted. "We better stop this, they will be home soon," Sidney said. Sidney removed her hand from Reagan's sweet spot, gave her one last kiss, and let her get up. Reagan tried to stand but was too weak. She felt as though all of the energy had been sucked right out of her body and replaced with a vigorous tingling sensation. It was the most amazing feeling Reagan had ever felt.

"We better go to the family room and watch TV before they get back," Sidney said. "Go to the guest bathroom and wash up, and I'll wash up in here, grab us a couple of cold drinks and meet you up front."

Reagan and Sidney continued to have those explosive encounters every time Reagan came to visit Brea. It was something Reagan felt she needed at the time because it made her feel normal. Even though being with Sidney intimately made Reagan feel normal, she still struggled with it spiritually. Reagan hated the fact that she couldn't tell anybody about her feelings, let alone her encounters with her special friend.

The next year, Sidney was leaving for college and told Reagan they should no longer have sex. Sidney wanted to get to know the college girls and didn't want Reagan getting in the way. Reagan cried and begged her to reconsider and to keep her around as her hometown girlfriend. Deep down Reagan felt used, that Sidney had used her for the past year and was now ready to replace her for the next best "college girl."

She concluded that we sometimes confuse a person's act of selfishness as an act of caring for us and that it's easier to accept this than admitting the truth of false love.

Once Sidney got to college, she totally came out of the closet. She was always on social media posting pictures of herself and different girls. When she came home for breaks and some weekends, she would always deem it necessary to tell Reagan about all of her various girlfriends, totally unaware of how much this hurt Reagan. The only time Sidney spent with Reagan was sneaking around to have sex during her school breaks. Reagan didn't even care, she settled for whatever time she could get to make her feel loved. Sidney stopped calling to check up on Reagan, or texting to let her know she was just thinking about her.

Reagan was about to experience a pain that exceeded all the hurts she'd ever felt before. One particular Thanksgiving break, Sidney decided to bring one of her girlfriends' home with her for the holiday. Since Sidney's parents were aware of her sexual preference this was okay with them.

That weekend, Reagan invited herself to spend the weekend with Brea, as she always did when she knew Sidney would be home. When Brea and Reagan walked into the family room, Reagan could not believe her eyes.

There was Sidney sitting on the love seat, with a beautiful

young lady snuggled close to her, facing her, and they were

gazing into each other's eyes. She watched them softly

kiss, followed by moments of gazing at each other some

more. Sidney was stroking the girl's hair. They were so

mesmerized with one another that they had no idea Brea

and Reagan had even walked in the room.

"Oh, my god!" Brea yelled. "It's bad enough they

let you bring this mess into the house but I refuse to watch

you make out, Sidney! Just because mama and daddy aren't

here doesn't mean you can do that stuff out here in the

family room! Goodness! Come on, let's go to my room

Reagan."

Brea grabbed Reagan by the arm and dragged her

towards her room.

"She makes me sick!" Brea exclaimed, turning to

look at her friend. "What's wrong with you, Reagan?"

Reagan was dripping with sweat; her knees were weak, her heart pounding hard and fast. She could feel a hurt deep in the pit of her stomach and there was a knot the size of a baseball in the back of her throat. Reagan couldn't believe Sidney would ever bring another girl in her face like this. She was holding her as she'd always held Reagan, kissing her like she kissed Reagan. The young lady had long dark-brown hair, light mocha skin complexion, and dark brown eyes. She was from India and absolutely gorgeous.

Reagan had suppressed her feelings and desires for women for years, abandoned by her father, molested, raped, physically and mentally abused, and spiritually confused. She had taken all those feelings that were tormenting her and bottled them up in her relationship with Sidney where she felt safe. And to now open her eyes and come to the reality of it ending put everything heavily back on her shoulders.

That night Sidney spent every moment with her new girlfriend and never even looked Reagan's way. That Saturday morning Reagan went to the kitchen for a bowl of cereal. To her surprise, Sidney and her girlfriend were already at the table sharing a bowl of fruit and yogurt parfait.

"Good morning," Reagan said.

There was no answer. Instead, the young lady looked over at Reagan, and mumbled something under her breath, followed by a burst of laughter. Reagan looked over at Sidney, feeling betrayed and hurt.

"Cut it out!" Sidney said to her girlfriend.

"*I'm sorry, but I just can't believe you didn't know that you were committing statutory rape,*" the girl said, sarcastically.

←CHAPTER FOUR→
Straw House

The summer after graduating from high school was very scary for Reagan. She didn't want to go to college. She didn't have a real job. She was a cashier at a local burger joint not too far from her house so she walked to work most days.

She really wanted to join the Navy but, ironically, she allowed her mom to talk her out of the idea.

"If you join the military, you will become a lesbian." Her mom said.

Reagan always felt her mom knew but was in denial because her mom has always had intuitions about things. But if she did, she never spoke on it.

Being raised as a Christian, Reagan was taught homosexuality was an abomination to God. She tried very hard to fight her feelings and hated herself for being attracted to girls. She sometimes found herself being very mean to and picking fights with girls she found attractive. This made her a loner and she spent a lot of time to herself. In fact, she still has introvert issues to this day. As a child and into high school she never had a boyfriend but did develop a huge crush on one boy in high school. It was right after Sidney went away for college and Reagan figured out she liked him because he reminded her so much of Sidney.

Like Sidney, he was passionate about sports. Reagan tried hard to focus all her thoughts on him, convinced that if she had feelings for him and tried to forget about Sidney, then maybe she wouldn't be a lesbian anymore. Reagan really didn't want to be a lesbian. Everybody around her made her feel like gays and lesbians were not only going to hell but were mentally ill and abnormal people.

There was a lesbian couple with kids that lived in her neighborhood and all the "normal" moms forbade their children to go anywhere near their house. They made the kids feel as though those women were child molesters, despite their Bible clearly teaching them to show love. Some "Christians" say hate the sin and love the person, but their actions don't line up with what the Bible reads in Romans 5:8 *"But God demonstrates his love for us while we were still sinners."*

Eventually Reagan did come out to her family, friends, and church members. But one thing she noticed was that some of the "church folk" who followed her on social media no longer "liked" or commented on anything she posted after they found out she was a lesbian. Some even" un-followed" her, even if the post had nothing to do with promoting the gay lifestyle. Just knowing that she was a lesbian and they hadn't seen her "in church" any more meant they couldn't support her with likes or comments.

Unfortunately, Reagan's guy crush didn't work out anyway because he never had any type of feelings for her and she totally wasn't his type. Let's just say, no black girl was his type. Needless to say, there she was once again let down by another male in her life.

In efforts to stay "saved," Reagan avoided friendships with girls because of her feelings and fear of what she knew it could lead to. Also, after being made to feel rejected and unloved as a child, she feared being rejected by straight women. Also, she didn't want to offend them by crossing the line. This made suppressing her feelings make more sense to her, though still painful.

Reagan's plan out of high school was to get married and have kids. She figured if she started a family, she could possible stay straight. One day when Reagan was working the front cash register at the burger joint, two guys she'd never seen before walked in. One of them walked up to her register and placed his order. When she gave him his total he handed her his money along with a note that read:

"Hi my name is Cass I've been working in the area for a little over a month but today is my last day in the area. I didn't want to leave without giving you my number. I would've spoken to you sooner but you're always so busy when I come in. I'm looking forward to your call my number is..."

Cass and Reagan got to know each other pretty quickly and spent most of their time together. Even though Reagan knew deep down she had no interest in men, she felt like this was something she had to do. In order to please God, she had to be with a man. She had to sacrifice and suppress her feelings because what she was feeling was wrong.

Cass and Reagan got married less than a year later. They gave birth to their first child, Justin, a year after that.

Their two girls, Cassidy and Cassandra, quickly followed Justin. Reagan struggled with her sexuality everyday throughout the marriage. Cass would always question her about why she didn't have any female friends. He couldn't understand why his wife could never connect with the girlfriends and wives of his male friends. Reagan viewed her situation the same as an addiction. You wouldn't expose a drug addict to drugs so she didn't want to expose herself to getting too close to women. She was a firm believer; if you play with fire you will get burned.

Reagan began to pray and ask God to send her a good female friend, one she could call her sister. She needed this not because of Cass, but for herself. She was beginning to feel overwhelmed with everything she was holding inside and needed a friend she could trust.

One night Cass came home all excited about a friend of his he'd bumped into earlier that day.

"Friday night we are going to their house to watch a boxing match, I really want you give his wife a chance," he said.

"Honey, you know I don't get along with women too well, but okay, I'll try," she responded.

They pulled up to the couple's house that night and boy was is it nice! They had two elegant vehicles in the driveway - a white on white Mercedes AMG E63 S and a Mercedes G-Class SUV, same color. Cass rang the doorbell and an amazingly beautiful and spunky young lady opened the door.

"Hello there, I'm Sonji! Come on in!" she exclaimed.

She was wearing a pair of tight, perfectly fitted, ash blue jeans with a designer hole on the left thigh, a low V-cut blouse that fit tight around her waist and body, a big brown belt, and brown boots. She had on a silver choker and large silver hoop earrings, both from Tiffany's. Her makeup was flawless, and beat to the Gods; it was natural toned to match her light caramel skin. Her hair was natural, long and looked to be freshly flat-ironed. It hung just below her shoulders and was colored honey blonde.

At first, Reagan thought God was playing a joke on her. She prayed and asked him for a female friend that she could truly be friends with and only have feelings as a sister for. And then he places this fine-assed woman with all the traits Reagan was attracted to in her life! Reagan loved petite females with their own hair (no weave), big pretty eyes, nice white teeth who were spunky but soft spoken, a woman willing to allow Reagan to take control and protect her, yet put Reagan in her place when needed.

"God, you got jokes!" Reagan said to herself.

The truth of the matter is that sometimes we profess things to be blessings or sent by God that didn't even come from God. We have to learn to wait and understand the purpose for someone being in our life and not move too fast.

Sonji and Reagan hit it off right away. Reagan had landed a great job working in logistics and got Sonji hired on, too. They were literally together every day. If they weren't working, shopping, or at each other's house, they would talking on the phone. However, the more time they spent together, the deeper Reagan's feelings for Sonji went in the wrong direction.

Reagan had the husband and kids; yet, she found it even harder to fight her sexual desires for women and, more importantly, Sonji. No matter what she did with her husband and kids to get her mind off her desires, her mind was always on Sonji. It became so overwhelming until her feelings literally began to show on the outside. Sonji eventually picked up on Reagan's feelings towards her.

One morning, Reagan came into work and found out Sonji had quit the job she helped her land. This was very strange because Sonji really liked the job and was doing quite well there.

That evening when Reagan got home from work, she gave Sonji a call to find out what was going on. Reagan was shocked and speechless at what Sonji had to say:

"We are spending way too much time together, and it's not healthy," she explained. "I feel our time has run its course, I'm not sure what's going on, but it's making me feel very uncomfortable.

"I do not understand your neediness to be around me so much, nor do I like this vibe I'm feeling from you," Sonji went on. "Yes, I made the decision to walk away from that good job because I'm woman enough to remove myself from any situation that can potentially cause harm to my family or me."

She continued, "I think you need to be honest for your family. Notice how I didn't say be honest for yourself, because I think you already know the truth. But you need to be honest for your husband and kids. You are playing a dangerous game with the people in your life.

I'm hanging up the phone now and I ask that you not ever call me again."

Then she hung up the phone, not allowing Reagan to utter one word.

Reagan was devastated, ashamed, and heartbroken. She secretly cried for days and could barely eat anything. She couldn't believe what she'd heard. Sonji had picked up on her feelings, and intentions. Instead of sticking around to work through it with Reagan - her friend, her sister - Sonji walked out of Reagan's life, never to see or speak with her again.

It was shocking because Reagan had been successful for so long at keeping anyone from noticing. She had never made any advances towards her; yet, she still knew. No one had ever called Reagan out like this before. The funny thing about it was she actually felt relieved that someone knew, even if that someone had just broken her heart, and walked out of her life.

Cass loved Reagan dearly and Reagan never doubted that at all. Unfortunately, she was only with him in body only. Her heart and spirit were never in this relationship for the reasons they should've been. She held on for two reasons only: one was the love she finally received from a man that she lacked and longed for from her father, and, two, to be "right" with God and not burn in hell. But the love she had for Cass was the love one would have for their best friend. He was the best thing in Reagan's life during that time, but was that fair to him?

Sometimes Reagan would cry during sex with Cass because she could feel the love he had for her and she knew she didn't feel the same for him. Sex with Cass always reminded her of when she was molested as a child. Because of her real preference, it made her feel as if she was being forced to do it and it just didn't feel natural. Reagan knew deep in her heart she wasn't supposed to be there; she longed to touch the softness of a woman.

Sometimes after sex Reagan would wait until Cass fell asleep, then close her eyes and masturbate. She would imagine the touch, and smell of a woman. When she got really lucky and had the house to herself, she would masturbate while watching lesbian porn. Masturbation became more and more frequent for Reagan. It seemed to be the solution to her problem. By privately masturbating, she could continue to fake her happiness and fool those around her.

Deep inside her heart she was a very unhappy young lady, even though she knew Cass loved her. Reagan also knew there was a whole other life out there that she desired to live and she just couldn't seem to let that go.

The young couple had other problems in our marriage, too. Cass wasn't perfect. He struggled with keeping a job and a roof over his family's head. During their marriage, he never held a job for any length of time.

He would work a few months and come home with a story on how the boss didn't like him.

Reagan was a Capricorn so being successful on the job was very serious to her. So she could never understand why he didn't see it that way. Deep down, she hated him for his inability to keep a job. They lived paycheck-to-paycheck, trying to make ends meet. Coming home to find out the utilities were disconnected or that they were being evicted and had to move in with one of their parents became a normal routine. It certainly didn't help Reagan's ability to hold on to the marriage.

Reagan had to call her older brother Maurice once for assistance with their bills. His response would never leave her and actually weighed heavy on her mind. She thought about what he said when she finally got the courage to walk away and find her happiness. Maurice told her: *"I'm sorry but you can do bad by yourself."*

53

Reagan began to ask herself why… Why can't I be happy? Why should I put up with a man who doesn't seem to have the drive to sacrifice whatever he has to in effort to take care of his family? Why should I have to force myself to have sex with a person simply because it was a man? Why can't I find my happiness? Why am I abnormal just because of whom I love?

From Reagan's perspective, a person who is truly homosexual can't be delivered from it, because it's who they are. She felt that if a homosexual person went to a church, got prayer for deliverance from homosexuality, and they began living as a heterosexual, that's their decision and choice. They weren't "delivered" from homosexuality; they just chose to begin living as a heterosexual. Point being, they would still have feelings for the same sex, they would have to choose their situations wisely to not put themselves in any compromising situations, because they will still struggle with homosexuality. Consider this: if a heterosexual person with a sex addiction gets delivered from the addiction, they will still have those desires and no one could tell Reagan any different. It's just a matter of if they choose to act on those desires. Why do you think so many so-called "church folk" and preachers are caught up in sexual acts every other time you turn your TV on? Ask yourself this: would you allow a convicted child molester to spend time with your child alone after they were "delivered?" Of course you wouldn't; that's also why they have to register as sex offenders. It's believed that a child molester or sex offender is that for life. A heterosexual person is that way for life. But homosexuals are expected to believe they aren't normal and that they need to just put those feelings down and walk away from who they are. They are treated like sex offenders and child molesters, even when they are consenting adults minding their own business.

Reagan asked herself why she should stress herself out to make ends meet without support from her husband. She realized her brother was merely telling her *that your spouse or mate is supposed to help you, build you, and inspire you to do better in life rather than tear you down, take away from you, and drive you to a lower place in life. And if they are not bringing you to a happier place in life, why are you with them?* "You can do bad by yourself"

Reagan's family and friends would avoid them at gatherings because they were known to ask for money or a place to stay. Reagan even worked two jobs at one point and that still wasn't enough to cover all the bills. In retrospect, this should've made Reagan happy because she had the dominant role in the marriage.

Getting married before either of them turned twenty was not a good idea at all. Cass still needed to learn the value and importance of maintaining a job and taking care of his family. Reagan, on the other hand, really should've waited to make sure she knew what she was getting into.

Giving up what her heart truly desired, she was destined to

fail, not to mention that she was playing with Cass's heart

along the way. It was a stupid and dangerous thing for her

to do. When you take a trip by plane the first thing the

flight attendant says is, to put your mask on first. Why do

they tell you that? Because how can you help others if you

need help yourself?

One night after coming home late and tired from her

second job, Reagan was extremely exhausted. She took a

long, hot bubble bath and actually dozed off in the tub.

Cass woke her up and told her she needed to come to bed.

Moments later, she climbed into bed expecting to go right

to sleep but, of course, Cass got started rubbing, kissing,

and trying to take her panties off. Reagan became very

angry, and was finding it harder and harder to be intimate

with him, especially when he was out of work or if she felt

stressed over the bills. But this particular night, she was just too tired for sex and wasn't in the mood at all.

"Not tonight honey," Reagan said.

Cass became very angry by this and began to yell and swear at his wife.

"What is your fucking problem? "Are you fucking someone else?" he asked.

"NO!" Reagan shouted, "I'm just tired. I did just work two jobs tonight, you know."

Cass then placed his hands around her neck, squeezing it tightly. "You're going to make me do something I'll later regret, because I don't believe you!" he screamed. He then let out a loud roaring sound, squeezing harder and not letting go of her neck until he got his full roar out. Reagan began coughing uncontrollably, trying to get air back into her lungs as Cass jumped out of bed, threw his clothes on and ran out of the apartment.

Reagan laid in bed crying and afraid, not knowing what to do but realizing that now more than ever some changes had to be made. She prayed to God, "Lord, I need your help".

Reagan hadn't told anyone of her attraction to women except for Sidney; Sonji had figured it out on her own. Up to this point, she'd contemplated telling Cass several times before. After tonight, she was sure he wasn't ready and couldn't handle knowing. She tossed and turned for a while that night, deep in thought because she knew change was inevitable.

The next morning Cass was home, back in bed holding his wife close in his arms. She could hear his heart beating as he slept peacefully. She knew deep in her heart this man truly loved her. How could she hurt him with the truth about who she really was? Wouldn't it be very selfish of her to disclose her true feelings and walk away from this marriage? Reagan was torn because she felt like she was supposed to sacrifice her feelings and desires for her three beautiful children. What she didn't want was for her children to ever be without their father as she had been.

Then there was the spiritual side of it. Reagan truly loved going to church, especially praise and worship, because it enabled her to disengage herself from everybody and connect one on one with God. The problem was the "church folk" mentality. They had a way of making you feel unwanted or that you didn't belong there. It reminded Reagan of a video that went viral on social media. The caption read: "Preacher slaps demon out of woman." This preacher slaps the poor woman with all of his power over and over, from one cheek to the other, her face turning extremely red from his blows. Reagan was not sure what the preacher felt the woman's issue was, but she couldn't help but wonder just how many "church folk" would love to do that to homosexuals, based on how they treat them. No one would be surprised.

Reagan and Cass divorced after nine years; there were just too many issues in the marriage. Reagan, being a very strong-minded and dominant female found it hard to see a weak man who could not take control of his family. From her perspective, their house was definitely made of *straw*.

←CHAPTER FIVE→
Doing Too Much

After the divorce, Reagan began to live a bisexual life. She had gotten up the courage to tell her closest cousin, but for the most part Reagan was still "in the closet" and didn't want certain people in her life knowing that she slept with women.

Reagan did meet a true female friend named Chari, who is like a sister to her even to this day. She was Justin's preschool teacher but they hit it off from the start as true friends. She accepted Reagan for who she was and kept her secret even though people started rumors about the two of them. She was never ashamed of Reagan, which gave

Reagan a strong love for their friendship. As a child,

Reagan always wanted a sister and she was exactly that.

Reagan made a point to tell Chari about her sexual desires

towards women very early in their friendship. Reagan

wanted this friendship to work therefore she had to trust

Chari with her truth.

Reagan went from one fling to another - men,

women - it just didn't matter to her. She continued dating

men to keep people from figuring out her secret. Cass

would get the kids every other weekend, giving Reagan the

opportunity to hit the streets in search of companionship.

She would hit the straight clubs one weekend and the gay

clubs the next. Reagan took pride in the fact that both men

and women wanted her. She always had an athletic build

and worked out daily to keep herself-looking good, not to

mention her big brown eyes and bright smile that would

brighten up any room.

On one of Reagan's "straight club" nights, she was

sitting alone at a table having a drink. She must've drifted off in her thoughts because when she looked up this extremely handsome young man was at her table. He was wearing a tight fitting shirt exposing all of his cuts as his shirt hung perfectly on his body. Reagan has a thing for fit bodies, male or female. He had a naturally curly Mohawk haircut and a nicely groomed beard. He looked to be mixed race and was super gorgeous!

"What you drinking on beautiful?" he asked. "Mind if I sit?

Reagan gave him a slight smile and motioned her hand for him to have a seat.

"Well, what you drinking?" He asked.

"Oh, it's a Long Island," Reagan said with a laugh.

"Dang girl! You going strong tonight, aren't you?" You've already put down three of em'." he said, smiling. "Let me order you another one.

"I've been watching you for a minute, and I see

you're alone and might need a designated driver tonight," he continued, "and I can't bear the thought of a lovely woman like you not making it home safely."

"Dude, I don't even know your name. Let's start with that," Reagan said. "Plus I have an Uber account," she said, holding up her cell phone.

"Oh! Where are my manners? My name is Carlos but everybody calls me Los," he said.

"Oh, okay. I'm Reagan. Nice to meet you, Los," Reagan said.

That night, they talked for hours and Reagan had a few more Long Islands. He only had one drink so she decided to take him up on his offer to give her a ride home. Reagan was on a tight budget, saving for a house for her and her kids. She'd purchased a small three-bedroom townhouse as a starter home about thirty-five minutes west of downtown Atlanta. Reagan punched her address into Los's car GPS system, laid back on the seat and closed her eyes. It was a nice ride from the city. He drove a brand-new, red Mustang. The sound of the engine roaring as they coasted down I-20 west was soothing to Reagan.

"Can I ask you a question?" he asked.

"What!" Reagan moaned half asleep.

"Why are you drinking so much? No woman as beautiful as you should drink that much," he said. "And though I'm happy to be here for you, you should never put yourself in this kind of situation where a stranger is driving you home."

Reagan seemed to drink more on her straight club nights. When she went to the gay clubs she spends most of her time watching all the beautiful ladies. It was almost like she was using the alcohol to fill a void at the straight clubs. She's passed out in more strange places than she'd ever admit to.

One night, Reagan got drunk in a straight club and flirted with a young lady who was there with her man. The guy had a few choice words for Reagan, and she mouthed

back at him. Before she knew it, the guy popped her in the

nose. The damage to Reagan's nose required surgery to

repair. Ironically, the young lady Reagan took the punch

for came to visit her in the hospital. They hooked up a

couple of times after that but it was nothing serious.

"Oh, my god! First, you're a fucking knight in

shining armor trying to save a bitch and now you're trying

to be a daddy to a bitch!" Reagan exclaimed indignantly.

"Nigga, I don't know my piece of shit daddy, never have,

and likely never will, so I ain't trying to start having one

now, I'm good over here."

"Okay, sorry for caring," Los said.

Reagan had fallen asleep by the time they pulled

into her driveway.

"Reagan, wake up," Los said with a whisper. He

helped her into the house.

"Come on up to my room, you can spend the night,"

Reagan said. "There is no need for you to get back on the road this time of night. Besides, I'll need you to take me to get my car in the morning."

"Are you sure?" he asked.

"Yeeesss!!!" Reagan said, irritation showing in her voice. "Man, are you always this annoying? I said you could stay, didn't I? Reagan asked with sarcasm.

"Come on!" Reagan demanded, stomping up the stairs.

Reagan was an early bird so she woke up before Los that morning with her face buried in his chest. She looked up at him as he slept so peacefully. His cologne smelled good. He had his arms around her, making her feel safe. She lay there for a little while longer, listening to his heartbeat as he slept. It was during this time of her life when she realized this was exactly what she wanted from a man - she wanted him to be strong and give her a sense of security, a safe haven.

Reagan wanted men to give her the protection, love, and affection she never received from her father. She always dreaded the moment when they wanted to have sex with her. She could cuddle with them all day as long as they didn't mention sex. She loved going out with men, watching sports, and talking to them, but having sex with them was her only issue.

Although Los seemed to be so perfect the night Reagan met him, she later found out that he had a girlfriend and a son at home. He never seemed to spend time with his son, which bothered Reagan. Because of how her dad abandoned her, it was very important to Reagan for men to spend time with their children. Los was also a heavy marijuana smoker. Needless to say, Reagan slowly began to back out of the relationship. The last conversation Reagan had with Los, he told her she needed to put out more sexually.

Because she was a single mother of three, no man would stick around long if her sex game were not on point. Los felt that no man would ever consider Reagan as "wifey" material because of her three kids and that they would date her as long as she was putting out. He told her they would then move on once they found the right one for them. Basically she would only serve as a temporary girl to any man.

Reagan really didn't care if what he said was true or not because she had no desire to marry another man anyway, but the fact he said those things to her made Reagan feel worthless, and very angry.

Reagan learned quickly after her divorce that false love always gives sight. She began to realize how the signs were always there and how she was the one choosing to ignore them. It actually became quite entertaining watching people come in and out of her life and transition from audition mode to who they really were. She would always remember what her mom told her, "It was only an audition".

Reagan usually spent her Sundays hanging out with her best friend, Chari, and her family. This gave her a sense of normalcy. Chari had the perfect family: a loving husband, Lane, whom she loved, and their three boys. Their family ran like a well-oiled machine. They really worked well together making the marriage work. They understood one another's needs and made sacrifices for the good of their marriage.

For example, Lane absolutely loved to play baseball and played in a league for the city. Chari understood this and supported him, making sacrifices for him to enjoy this outlet that pulled him away from the family. Chari, on the other hand, needed some time to herself away from her usual duties at home. Therefore, Lane allowed her to have her ladies' night out with a few of her friends, all straight of course. Reagan would go with them sometimes but none of them knew of her sexual preference except Chari.

Their ladies' nights out included shopping, going to the spa, getting their nails done, sitting down to a nice dinner, and going to the movies. The group of women even started a book club. Reagan enjoyed going to the book club meetings. The other women enjoyed Reagan as well because she would recite one of her poems for them. Reagan started writing in middle school. She was actually really good at spoken word too. Lane would watch the boys one night a month so his wife could enjoy her outlet.

Chari always took Reagan's visits as opportunities to lecture her and voice her concerns regarding her promiscuous lifestyle. Now, Chari didn't judge Reagan for having an interest in women; she was only concerned about the manner in which she went about it. Chari knew all of Reagan's secrets and the various partners she was dealing with.

"So let me get this straight, this new chick' you're messing with has a live in boyfriend, right? Are you crazy? What if he catches you over there?" Chari asked on one occasion.

"He's not going to catch me, "Reagan answered, trying to convince her friend. "Besides, he's a business traveler and flies out of town every week. He's miles and miles away.

"Trust me I got this," Reagan said, with confidence.

"Okay, you got this… you really need to be careful is all I'm saying; you are truly playing with fire this time," said Chari.

She continued, "I just don't understand you sometimes; you act like you don't care about the value of your life. What about your kids? I know the right person is out there for you, so stop kidding yourself, listen Reagan, if you want a woman, then wait for her.

"I'm just worried about you, *Mija*. What happens when one of your many lovers has a jealous rage on you? You've seen snapped!"

Reagan sat on a kitchen stool watching Chari as she perfectly cut small cubes of potatoes and placed them in a pot of water. Chari and her family are of Latin decent and she loves to cook for her family. She always made Reagan and her kids sit down and eat with them when they visited. Because she knew Reagan hated cooking and would feed the kids TV dinners most nights. Chari was talking a mile a minute, never taking her eyes off her task at hand or allowing Reagan to speak.

"I know you don't want to hear this, but you're like a sister to me," she added.

"My boys call you Auntie, and we don't want to see anything happen to you. You are our family," Chari said, with affirmation.

"I understand everything you're saying, but you got to understand my position, too," said Reagan.

"Coming out is not an option for me right now."

"There are just too many people who won't understand it."

"And you're right, I can't commit to a man because, well *hello* - been there done that!"

"I already know that won't make me happy."

"I refuse to live my life in misery, for the satisfaction of others ever again." Reagan explained.

"Just last month, that girl tracked you down at another chick's house and keyed your car," Chari pointed out.

"Then let's not forget about the guy you went out with from your job," Chari said.

"You trusted him enough to crash on your couch after hanging out late. Reagan, *he raped you!*"

"And you wouldn't even report it to the police."

"Heck you didn't even report him to your job so they could at least fire his ass!"

75

"All I'm saying is changes gotta be made Reagan."

Chari advised.

"I tell you what, find a good woman, for God's sake, who

will understand your situation and only see her." She said.

"But you've got to stop going the way you are." "Right

now, you are *doing entirely too much!*"

←CHAPTER SIX→
True Love

Reagan decided to take heed to what Chari had to say. She broke off all relationships and began to focus on herself and the kids. She spent most of her time getting the kids involved in extracurricular activities. Justin played basketball, football, and in the band; Cassidy was a writer and dancer; and Cassandra was a dancer and cheerleader.

Reagan and the girls were at one of Justin's basketball games. Reagan would occasionally take a glance over to check on Cassidy and Cassandra playing with two other little girls just below her on the bleachers.

During one of her fixations on the game, she heard a loud bang followed by a cry. She turned around and one of the little girls, who looked to be about three years old, lost her footing on the bleachers, and fell hitting her head pretty hard on the bleacher. Reagan jumped up, ran down the bleachers, picked the little girl up and began comforting her. She looked around to see if she saw a frantic mom headed her way and sure enough there she was.

She was very upset but seemed to be more angry than anything.

"I told you to stop jumping and running on these bleachers!" she yelled! "You're okay. Stop that crying right now!" The young lady demanded.

"I think she's mostly scared" Reagan said, with a slight smile. "I checked and there's no bump or anything on her head."

The little girl had her arms clinched tightly around Reagan's neck. She had stopped crying for the most part, except for the sniffles. Reagan sat down and put her on her lap to get a little more comfortable, and took a cloth out of her backpack and began wiping the little girl's face. You will never catch Reagan without her backpack.

"What's your name?" asked Reagan.

"Lindan," the little girl murmured with what little breath she had left.

"Lindan?" asked Reagan, with a smile. "That's a pretty name!"

Lindan put her head down and laid it comfortably on Reagan's chest.

"Oh, my gosh, she's loving this! She's already spoiled enough," her mother said, shaking her head.

"It's no problem at all. I love kids," Reagan said. "By the way, I'm Reagan."

"Oh, my name is Brooklyn. Nice to meet you!" The girl's mother said.

"No, the pleasure is all mine," assured Reagan.

After the game Reagan walked Brooklyn to her car, mainly because Lindan was still sleeping in her arms. Plus she didn't want to leave without exchanging phone numbers. Brooklyn was the first person that took her mind off Basketball and actually kept her entertained on conversation alone. Reagan carefully placed Lindan in her car seat, and buckled her in and softly closed the door.

"Thank you so much," Brooklyn said.

"You're quite welcome," Reagan said. "So, what brings you to a youth basketball game? You got a son on one of the teams?" Reagan asked.

"Ha-ha, no. Lindan is my only child," Brooklyn explained. "We came to see my nephew Malcolm play." He went home with one of his teammates. My sister and I try to make sure one of us is in the stands. My parents try to support as much as they can but they stay very busy at church. Said Brooklyn rolling her eyes.

"Oh, okay. Here, take my card and give me a call sometimes. Maybe we can set up a play date for the girls soon," Reagan suggested.

"Sure, sounds good, I will do that," Brooklyn said.

Reagan headed back to her car, where the kids were waiting. She knew they would be hungry by now, and began mentally preparing herself for them fighting over what they would have for lunch. Dang! I should've invited them to lunch with us, she thought to herself.

A few days went by and still no call from Brooklyn. Man, I don't know why I'm trippin' over this chick, I don't even know if she's a lesbian or not. Reagan thought. Plus she mentioned something about her parents being busy with church. Maybe she's a Christian. She had all the physical attributes Reagan was attracted to. She was a lot shorter than Reagan, had her own natural hair, petite build, and beautiful eyes. She seemed to really take care of herself, and more importantly her child. She was very feminine, and Reagan just couldn't get that big, bright smile of hers out of her head.

Reagan waited anxiously all day to get home from work, help the kids with their homework, have dinner, get baths done, and put them to bed before the start of college basketball game on TV. The UNC Tar Heels were playing tonight and she had become a huge fan after doing a report on them in high school.

About five minutes into the first half of the game, Reagan received a phone call from a number she didn't recognize. She was both hesitant and irritated to answer because she didn't talk on the phone when the Tar Heels were playing. She finally picked up the phone on the third ring.

"Hello?"

"I'm sorry, did I wake you?" asked the sweet sounding, familiar voice. It was Brooklyn!

"Oh no, of course not," Reagan replied.

Whenever Reagan didn't recognize the number calling she would always answer the phone in her "sleepy voice." (If she answered the phone at all.)

"I was just watching a little TV. How are you doing tonight?" Reagan asked.

"I'm doing exceptionally well tonight," said Brooklyn. "Exceptionally?" asked Reagan.

"Yes! I got a promotion at work so I'm really excited about that," she said.

"Well congratulations!" said Reagan. "We need to go celebrate then."

"That would be nice," Brooklyn replied. "But first, I was calling to invite you all to Lindan's birthday party this coming weekend. Think you can come?" "I'm sorry for the short notice, but seeing how we just met and all. Brooklyn said with wit.

"Ha-ha yeah, this weekend? Hmmm, I think we can make that happen," Reagan replied. "Just text me the address and we're there."

"Okay great. I'll see you Saturday, and don't think you're getting off the hook from my promotion celebration," she said, as she laughed.

"Indeed!" replied Reagan.

"Talk to you later," Brooklyn said.

"Goodbye," said Reagan.

On Saturday mornings, Reagan usually slept in and usually didn't wake up until around ten, and even then didn't make it out of bed until eleven. This particular Saturday, the sound of a text message woke her up at six o'clock. She reached over to the vacant pillow beside her, with her eyes still shut, and grabbed her phone. Struggling to open her eyes, she fumbled through the cover, unlocked the phone, and read the message.

Today 06:00
Brooklyn:
Good Morning Reagan,
I'm so sorry for sending
this message so early.
I was afraid of getting
busy and not sending it
in time. Lindan's party
starts at 1:00 this
afternoon at LEGOLAND
3500 Peachtree Rd.
Atlanta, Ga. 30326
Looking forward to
seeing you guys there.

Reagan laid the phone down, threw the comforter over her head, and tried to fall back to sleep. She couldn't stop thinking about seeing Brooklyn again. I wonder if she would even be interested in dating a woman. What if she has a boyfriend, or even a husband? After dating the white girl with the live-in boyfriend, Reagan swore to her best friend Chari and herself she would never do anything like that again. Chari was always worried about Reagan during that time. The white girl's boyfriend was a business traveler, so during the kids' summer visits with their dad,

Reagan would spend the week with her while he was away. She lived in a 4,000 sq. ft. home worth over $500,000. It was the one time in Reagan's life she felt pampered and was spoiled by someone else. Reagan quickly realized she was being used for sex. The girl felt the passion was gone in her relationship and used Reagan for that lost spark. After Sydney Reagan was never the type to be in a using relationship, even if the using was mutual.

Reagan decided to sleep in for a few more minutes since she had plenty of time before having to get the kids up for the party. Reagan was very tired because she was up late trying to comfort a co-worker and friend, who looked up to her as a single mother. Reagan was a few years older than she so the young lady would come to her for advice from time to time. This time, it was extremely serious and Reagan didn't know exactly how to help her. The young single mother had two children, a ten-year-old son and a six-year-old daughter. She was twenty-seven years old and gave birth to her son at the age of seventeen.

The day before, the young lady came home early and her son was watching porn with his little sister. She beat her son pretty badly and destroyed the sex DVD he'd somehow gotten his hand on. She questioned her daughter to find out what all had gone on while she worked.

The young lady was here alone, her family lives in Cleveland but she moved to Atlanta because she went to school here and never went back to Cleveland. Not having family here sometimes gave her no other choice but to leave her kids home alone while she worked. Her daughter told her that her brother sometimes touched her down there and told her to touch him.

She was devastated and afraid of what she should do about it. No mother wants to turn her son over to the authorities, but at the same time, she must protect her daughter. In the end, Reagan advised her to find a close relative she could trust and get the boy out of the home for a while, and get both kids some counseling. Reagan's heart went out to the young lady and could only pray to God that she would never have to make a decision like that herself.

The alarm startled Reagan; it was now 11:00 in the morning. "Dammit! I must've fallen back to sleep, I didn't mean to sleep this long," she said. "Oh, well, let's get it." It was something she always said for self-motivation or if she didn't know what to expect about a situation. She got up and went to the bathroom to get herself together. She would wake the kids up afterwards. They were going to be all too excited about the going to the birthday party.

The kids were indeed very anxious about the party, and were all out talking to each other about what they were going to do when we got there. Reagan took the liberty to bring Chari's boys to the party with her, which meant she had a total of five kids with her. She was actually quite good with them and they all enjoyed spending time with her. Reagan was the fun one to be around. The boys especially enjoyed how she blasted her rap music in her car, bass bumping and all. Reagan and Chari kids really thought they were cousins for real and no one could tell them different. They truly loved each other.

They pulled into LEGOLAND at 12:30. Reagan was always on time and being late was one of her pet peeves, maybe because she was a Capricorn. She decided to shoot Brooklyn a text to see if she was there yet.

Today: 12:33
Reagan:
*What's up? We're in
the parking lot. Are you
here yet?*

Reagan clicked send and couldn't wait to get a reply. She was interested to see if Brooklyn was there yet or running late. While she waited for Brooklyn to reply to her text, she decided to hop out of the car and grab the five gifts from the trunk that she'd stopped by the toy store and let the kids pick out for Linden. She began to hand each one of them their gift to take into the party. "And don't take them out of the bag, either!" She said to each as she handed them off. She got back in the car and looked at the time on the display and it was 12:45, and still no response from Brooklyn. Five minutes later she heard the text tone on her phone.

Today: 12:50
Brooklyn:
Girl… everything is going wrong today. I'm on my way but, it will be like 20 minutes. Can you grab some sodas and Ice from that store across the street?

Reagan:
No prob.

Reagan took a deep breath and let out a long and slow sigh. She was thinking about how all of her relationships would start out with her buying things for women. What gives them the nerve, freedom, or okay to ask me stuff like this? I just met this woman and she's asking me to buy sodas and ice for her daughter's birthday party, Reagan thought. It's just crazy how some people can discern the kindness in a person and take advantage of them.

As Reagan pulled back into the parking lot, she noticed Brooklyn walking into the building with a crowd of people with her, mostly kids. She looked over at the time on her car display and it was now 1:15. What am I getting myself into? Reagan wondered to herself. Being late for anything was totally unacceptable behavior as far as Reagan was concerned.

The party went great, well, at least for the kids; they had an absolute blast. It was a little uncomfortable for Reagan because this man kept staring at her. And would always seem to appear whenever she had any type of alone moments with Brooklyn. On one of his interruptions, Brooklyn introduced the man.

"Oh my gosh, I'm so sorry; where are my manners? Dad, this is my friend Reagan. Reagan, this is my dad, Samuel," she said.

"Hi, nice to meet you," said Reagan, with her hand extended. He simply acknowledged Reagan with a half-smile, the kind you give when you really don't want to speak to someone, never reaching for Reagan's hand in return. Reagan nervously withdrew her hand back to her side.

"She's the one I was telling you about dad that helped Lindan when she fell off the bleachers." Brooklyn explained. There was a dead silence.

Reagan decided to break the silence. "Oh, well. I'd better go check on the kids and start my round-up." "It's getting late, the boys' mom will kill me if I get them home too late." "They have Sunday school in the morning, and she don't play." Reagan said with a smirk on her face.

Brooklyn's father still didn't change the blank look on his face. Reagan awkwardly walked away to begin her dreaded "it's time to go" fight with the kids.

Later that night, Reagan was in her media room in which she named her "woman cave." She was lying back on her favorite power recliner, with a much-needed beer in her hand, and watching her Tar Heels on her 65-inch 4K TV. She began to drift off into her thoughts, wondering what Brooklyn was up to. There were a few moments during the party when she felt they had a connection with each other. She definitely felt something but just wasn't sure what it was right now. Man, I really wish I knew what the deal was with her pops though. I can't shake this feeling. What if this is the *real love* I've been waiting for. Reagan thought to herself.

During half time, Reagan made a quick trip to the bathroom, grabbed another beer, and decided to shoot Brooklyn a thank you text.

93

Today 22:00
Reagan:
*Hey, U!
Just wanted to
say thanks for
the invite, we
really enjoyed it!*

Today 22:01
Brooklyn:
Glad to hear. Busy?

Today 22:04
Reagan:
lol nope.

← CHAPTER SEVEN →
For The Love of The Game

Reagan and Brooklyn became extremely close over the next several months. Reagan was beginning to feel as if this was it; this was the relationship she had been waiting for since she was in her late teens. She felt so complete with Brooklyn. Everything about their relationship was so easy in terms of her past relationships, them, and their children. They were there for each other and uplifted each other.

Brooklyn supported Reagan when she decided to go back to school. Brooklyn would stay up late with Reagan making sure she completed her classwork assignments. Reagan helped Brooklyn with becoming more time conscious and getting out of debt. Reagan was really good with money. With Reagan's guidance Brooklyn even

95

purchased some rental property and making a nice monthly profit.

There was one issue in their relationship, and that was Brooklyn's father. Reagan finally found out why he stared at her the way he did at the party. You see, he was the senior pastor of a pretty big church in their community, a mega church. They were on TV and everything; their picture was on a huge billboard on I-20 east. Brooklyn's parents knew she struggled with homosexuality and felt they'd prayed and delivered her from the sin until she met Reagan. Brooklyn had shared all kinds of deliverance stories with Reagan on how her parents and church family would surround her and poured oil on her head while praying in tongues, pleading, and crying out to God for her deliverance. Brooklyn felt the need to suppress her feelings because she hated seeing her parents, especially her mom, go through this. Brooklyn didn't want to feel as though she was the cause of her mom's pain.

Reagan understood all too well how Brooklyn and her parents felt. She was raised in the same type of church and saw this happen to other members from the LGBT community during deliverance services. Reagan kept her feelings and desires hidden because of this.

Reagan made several attempts of suicide during her younger years. The pressure of holding all of her emotions in at such a young age, coupled with the possibility of seeing the pain and hurt of her mom and grandparents, made her secretly suicidal.

One night after one of the deliverance services, Reagan closed herself into the bathroom, grabbed the .38 caliber revolver that she'd sneaked from her grandfather's collection a few years before, and laid it on the bathroom counter. She stared at herself in the mirror with a heavy heart and tears welled up in her eyes. She always kept just one bullet in the cylinder. Reagan began to cry out to God; asking Him *why did you make me this way? Why do I have to feel so much pain?* She took the gun, placed it in her mouth, and clinched the barrel with her teeth. Squeezing her eyes closed tight, she pulled the trigger. *"Click"* went the gun. She opened her eyes, dropped to the floor and fell asleep crying.

Reagan had a lot of questions for God. She really wanted to know why he wouldn't let her end her life when she pulled that trigger? She overdosed on pills and vomited them back up fifteen minutes later. What was her purpose? With the failed attempts on her life, she felt like God was telling her that He loved her. She was Gods child just like she was and no longer had to be ashamed about it. God wanted her to have no guilt. After having that revelation Reagan began to feel better about herself. She was ultimately able to walk away from her marriage to Cass guilt-free because she knew God loved her even when no one else would.

Having the understanding of what Brooklyn was going through gave Reagan the courage to tell Brooklyn that she would be willing to walk away from the relationship if it would make Brooklyn and her parents happy. Brooklyn's happiness and peace of mind meant the world to Reagan. She didn't want to come between Brooklyn and her parents. Reagan was the type of person who would always put her wants and desires second to her mate's. Brooklyn got very upset with Reagan for making this offer, and told her it was out of the question.

Brooklyn shared a three-bedroom house with her older sister, Tasha, and Tasha's twelve-year-old son Malcolm, both of whom were so loving and accepting of Brooklyn. Malcolm was such a humble young man with a big heart for his little cousin, Lindan. He was protective of her and it was really cute to see them together. Malcolm was a gifted basketball player and that gave him an automatic place in Reagan's heart because of her love of the game, Heck, if it wasn't for Malcolm, Reagan would have never met Brooklyn. Tasha had to work that day and had asked Brooklyn to take Malcolm to his game.

It didn't take long for Justin and Malcolm to become very close friends, always begging to hang out to play basketball, and video games. Lindan enjoyed being around Cassidy and Cassandra. They made her feel like a big girl since they were much older than she. With the exception of Brooklyn's dad, everything was going perfect and they seemed to have such a nice little family unit together. Reagan was beginning to feel like she would be with Brooklyn forever.

It was like any typical weekend for Reagan when Cass had the kids. Reagan didn't have anything big planned for the weekend and this was intentionally done. She was extra careful not to make any plans with Brooklyn because this was the first weekend of March Madness and she was not missing her Tar Heels play. Brooklyn gave her a hard time about her ability to sit in the house all day watching sports. Linden's father was not in her life; like Reagan's dad he was a class-act deadbeat. Reagan felt bad about it but used it to get time away to watch sports because Brooklyn rarely had a free weekend without Lindan.

Reagan grabbed a beer from the mini fridge, flopped comfortably onto her power recliner, picked up the remote and powered up the entertainment center. Cass had just left with the kids and the house was quiet, just how she liked it before a game. *Oh, man!* Reagan thought to herself. *I haven't talked to Brooklyn since I left work; I better call her before the game starts and smooth things over, tell her that I'm staying in tonight. It's been a long and stressful week at work.* Reagan tried to convince herself as she called Brooklyn.

"Hello," Answered Brooklyn.

"Hey, Babe!" Reagan said, as if she was talking to a baby. Reagan knew Brooklyn smiled all over whenever she addressed her in this manner. And she needed all the help she could get.

"Whatcha' doin'?" Reagan asked.

"Waiting on you," Brooklyn answered in a quiet, low, sexy voice. At this point, Reagan's stomach got all tied up in knots, her armpits beginning to sweat. She was speechless and couldn't utter one word. "What does she mean she's waiting on me?" Reagan, frantically thought to herself.

"Hello?" Brooklyn asked.

"Ahh, yeah, I'm here," Reagan answered. Where's Lindan?" Reagan asked, hoping this wouldn't come across wrong and offend Brooklyn.

"She's with my parents," Brooklyn responded.

"Oh, okay.., okay..," Reagan said, trying to think of something quick. "So why don't you come here, where there's more privacy? Plus, you can give Tasha and Malcolm some mother-son time."

"Malcolm is with his dad, and Tasha went out with friends and we both know she won't be home anytime soon," Brooklyn, explained.

Reagan noticed the frustrated tone in Brooklyn's voice.

"Okay, ma. Give me an hour to shower and pack a bag, and I'll be there. It's your world, whatever you want, okay babe?" Reagan said, trying to assure Brooklyn. Reagan hung up the phone, blurted out several FUCKS! Took a quick shower, packed a bag and hit the road.

She pulled up at Brooklyn's house at about 6:45 pm. The Tar Heels tipoff was scheduled for 9:40 that night. Worst case, she could spend time with Brooklyn, pray she fell asleep early and then she could creep back downstairs and catch the Tar Heels. *I just got to work my magic and put her ass to sleep,* Reagan thought, a smile on her face. Reagan let herself in; they both had keys to each other's houses. As Reagan walked into the house, it became clear why Brooklyn wanted her to come over. She had an awesome aroma of spices coming from the kitchen. Brooklyn loved to cook; she always talked about writing her own cookbook one day. Reagan walked into the kitchen and dropped her keys and a bottle of wine on the counter. She looked up at Brooklyn, who was standing there with a sheer, see-through, red, thigh-length robe on, the silk belt untied. Her light caramel-toned body was glistening with oil. She was standing there, stirring a large, steaming pot. Never turning around, she said, "So, why did I feel as though you didn't want to come see me. Reagan?"

Without answering her lover, Reagan slowly walked up behind Brooklyn, placed her left hand between her thighs and slowly ran it up to her now wet pussy. She ran her right hand across Brooklyn's firm nipples. She could feel Brooklyn's body becoming limp, submitting to her will. Lightly rubbing her hand from her nipples to her chin, she tilted Brooklyn's head back resting it on her chest.

Reagan lightly tugged Brooklyn's hair to pull her head back further, making their lips meet, and began passionately kissing her.

Brooklyn dropped the spoon into the pot and turned to Reagan, giving herself to her totally. Reagan picked Brooklyn up, carried her over to a free countertop, and sat her down. Reagan began tenderly kissing Brooklyn's breast, stomach, and inner thighs, just enough to tease her and have her wanting more. Reagan knew it was working because Brooklyn's fingernails went deeper and deeper into Reagan's biceps as Brooklyn held on for dear life.

Reagan gave special attention to each nipple before working her way down Brooklyn's stomach to her inner thighs, Brooklyn let out a soft moan as her fingernails trailed up from Reagan's arms to the back of her neck and finally resting on the back of her head.

Reagan continued to glide her tongue in circular motions between Brooklyn's inner thighs, placing soft kisses and gentle bites as she worked her way to Brooklyn's wet pussy. Reagan could feel Brooklyn's pull on the back of her head. Reagan massaged Brooklyn's clit with the tip of her nose as she licked the outsides of Brooklyn's sweet and moist vagina. Reagan absolutely loved the smell and taste of Brooklyn's vagina. She'd even named Brooklyn's vagina "Pleasure".

"There's my pleasure," Reagan said, inhaling. At the very moment her tongue touched the tip of Brooklyn's clit, Brooklyn's phone rang. Brooklyn gently pushed Reagan's head away from pleasure.

"That's my dad's ringtone sweetie, I gotta answer it," Brooklyn said. She picked up the phone. "Hello daddy!"

Reagan poured each of them a glass of wine and took her glass to the living room to catch some of the earlier March Madness games while Brooklyn talked to her dad and finished up cooking.

As she watched the games, she drifted off into a daydream. Her mind was still on Brooklyn and Pleasure; no other woman's vagina had ever pleased her the way Pleasure did. Reagan named Brooklyn's vagina Pleasure because Brooklyn was the first person that gave her pleasure without touching her. She never considered herself a "Touch-Me-Not" lesbian, but she truly didn't need to be touched by Brooklyn to have an orgasm. Brooklyn was a very clean woman and ate all organic and healthy foods. Reagan believed this was a direct connection to Pleasure tasting so good; after all, you are what you eat, right?

Later that night after dinner, Reagan and Brooklyn were in the kitchen doing the dishes. Reagan noticed she had roughly fifteen minutes or so until tipoff of the Tar Heels game.

"So, what did your dad want? Everything okay with baby girl?" Reagan asked, trying to get her mind off the game.

"Oh, yeah, everything is cool. To be honest, I don't know what he wants. He has called me three times since I dropped Lindan off," Brooklyn, said.

"Huh, are you serious?" Reagan asked.

"Yeah, and it's beginning to weird me out. Every time he acts like this, something happens. You know he has the gift of discernment," Brooklyn said, matter of fact.

"Something like what!" Reagan asked.

"I don't know, sweetie, I just don't know," Brooklyn said. "Grab the wine, and bring it up to my room; I'm tired."

"You go on up. I'm going to stay down here for a while and watch the Tar Heels. They play tonight."

"What! Are you serious right now? Come, on sweetie, Pleasure needs you," Brooklyn pleaded.

"Babe, I'll make it up to you both, I'm only going to watch the first half, then I'll be up there," Reagan promised and kissed Brooklyn on the tip of her nose, then her forehead. "Babe just watch something on Netflix until I get up there." Reagan suggested.

"I'm just saying, this robe is coming off and I'm climbing in bed naked, and you want to stay down here to watch basketball?" said Brooklyn, as she sighed and stomped up the stairs.

Reagan lay on the couch, a part of her feeling bad for Brooklyn. She was torn, because she wanted Brooklyn and Pleasure just as bad; but on the other hand, she wanted desperately to see the game and her passion for the Tar Heels was just that deep. Brooklyn would understand, Reagan kept re-assuring herself.

Reagan was quite excited as her Tar Heels lead had swelled above 20 points with under a minute to go in the first half of the game. *I'll go on upstairs with my lady during halftime since it looks like we got this one locked down*, Reagan thought to herself. *Plus I'm not missing a play, as we get deeper into the tournament.* Reagan finished up her wine and waited for the final seconds to countdown in the half.

Reagan heard a click at the door as if someone had a key and unlocked it. It couldn't be Tasha because she usually comes through the garage door. "Who could it be?" Reagan wondered. Just as she stood up to head down the hall towards the door, she saw him standing there looking at her with that same cold, and blank look on his face. Reagan felt a dark fear overtake her body and emotions.

"What are you doing here?" The man asked. It was Brooklyn's father, Mr. Fletcher.

Reagan stood there, speechless and motionless. She could see and hear him but was unable to respond. Mr. Fletcher began slowly walking towards Reagan. As he stepped closer towards the light illuminating from the TV, Reagan could see he had something in his hand, pressed against his right leg. He took one more step, revealing what was in his hand: a large, shiny switchblade.

"Hold up! What's going on here, Mr. Fletcher?" Reagan exclaimed. Reagan, tried to keep her voice low, the last she wanted was to wake Brooklyn up to what was taking place in her living room. Mr. Fletcher pointed the blade towards Reagan.

"Have a seat, young lady. I'll ask the questions, starting with, what are you doing here?" Mr. Fletcher demanded. Only moving his lips, his teeth never parted.

"Sir, I'm a friend of Brooklyn, remember we met a Lindan's party last fall?"

Mr. Fletcher stared blankly at Reagan as if he was uninterested in what she had to say. After thinking up a quick lie, Reagan proceeded, "And, sir, I'm watching the game here because there's a power outage in my subdivision." She nervously pointed at the TV.

"Sit down!" Mr. Fletcher ordered.

Reagan slowly sat down on the couch, never taking her eyes off him.

111

"I know exactly who you are, and I know what's going on here," he said.

"Now, let me explain something to you," Mr. Fletcher said as he took a seat in the chair directly across from Reagan.

"My precious Brooklyn belongs to God. This lifestyle is not her destiny, not on my watch! I have come here to serve the devil notice, he *cannot* have my daughter," explained Mr. Fletcher, tears streaming down his face. Tears began to well up in Reagan's eyes also.

"Mr. Fletcher, God created your daughter, and he still loves her. There is nothing wrong with her. Don't you think God wants you to love all of his creations?" asked Reagan.

"My God did not create her to have inordinate affections such as this!" he argued. "I have come here tonight because He sent me, to take my daughter back by any means necessary!"

"But, sir, taking my life will not change how Brooklyn feels inside. Think of Brooklyn, sir. She truly loves me and there's no doubt in my mind about that," Reagan said.

Mr. Fletcher held his head in his hands. His tears were coming down pretty good and Reagan could see and feel his pain. He shook his head in agreement with Reagan.

"I know she loves you, she told me during the Christmas holidays. She said she didn't want to go another year without being free to express her love for you." Mr. Reagan said, grudgingly.

"She did?" Reagan asked with amazement.

"Yes, she did. That was the first time my precious Brooklyn admitted something to me she knew I didn't approve of, especially from a spiritual perspective," he said. "Wow, I don't understand. She never told me this. I wonder why she didn't tell me she'd told you this?" Reagan asked, confused.

"I don't know," He said, now staring at the floor. "I'm sorry it has to be this way, young lady, but I have a mission at hand and I must complete this mission. When Brook asked us to watch baby girl, I knew I'd find you here.

"She has never asked us to watch her; we have to ask for baby girl ourselves," he said. "I'm sure you're a nice girl, but I cannot have this demonic activity in my family." Mr. Fletcher stood up and began heading towards Reagan with the knife clinched in his hand.

"Wait a minute, Mr. Fletcher, please listen to me," Reagan said, now standing to defend herself.

Reagan began to silently pray. She remembered how her grandmother Lilly had taught her to call on Jesus in the time of adversity. She asked Jesus to help her to get out of this situation. She knew no matter what her sexual preference was, she still belonged to God. Here she stood eye to eye with a very powerful man of God, well known in the city of Atlanta. Yet, she was asking God to protect her against him.

"Listen, Mr. Fletcher, please hear me out," she began. "You yourself said Brooklyn loves me. How will she feel about you taking the life of the one she truly loves? Sir, I love you as I love Brooklyn, and I don't want to see you hurting. My promise to you is this: I will walk out of that door right now, never to return again."

Reagan pleaded, "Sir, I'm at your mercy. You don't want to do this, she will never forgive you. You don't want my blood on your hands." "Not only that, you are a Christian, and the main purpose of a Christian is to win souls to Christ." Reagan stated. "Am I right sir?" "Yes!" He answered.

"Then how will I get the opportunity to change if you take my life."

Mr. Fletcher fell to his knees, dropping the knife on the floor and began crying out to God, asking for forgiveness. Reagan quickly walked over and grabbed her keys from the coffee table. She stood there for a minute looking at Mr. Fletcher. He looked like a little boy crying to his father. She walked over to him and placed her right hand on the left side of his hunched shoulder and began to comfort him. She could feel his painful emotions release into her body. She felt very weak; her knees buckled, but she was able to keep her balance.

"Mr. Fletcher, sir, please never tell Brooklyn of this, I should be the one to break her heart, not you," she said. "And promise me to continue to protect and take care of Brooklyn and Lindan.

"And sir, please, as you carry out your ministry, please ask God to give you the ability to love every soul from where they are, because God is love," Reagan whispered.

She took her door key to Brooklyn's house off her key ring, laid it on the coffee table, turned and walked out the door.

The next several months were very hard. The task of breaking things off with Brooklyn took a huge toll on Reagan's spirit. Lying to her and convincing her she wasn't in love with her was the hardest thing she had to do. It was hard to see Brooklyn so hurt but Reagan knew this was the best way to handle this. She never wanted Brooklyn to have to choose between her and her parents. Because of the foundation that was instilled in her, Reagan was a very spiritual person. She knew it was only by God's grace she was able to speak to that man. From that night on, she had a testimony.

I'm thankful in knowing and understanding I still belong to God. He spared my life; He gave me the right words to say in the time of need. He spoke through me to an apostle of a mega church in Atlanta. He gave me the love of basketball, the Tar Heels, and had I not been watching that

game when Mr. Fletcher came to that house, he would've

caught me in bed with his daughter, I don't think I would

be here to tell this story right now had he seen that.

← CHAPTER EIGHT →
Living Life Abundantly

The experience with Mr. Fletcher really shook Reagan up and made her sit down and evaluate both her and her children's lives. Believe it or not, one of her biggest fears was for one of her children to sit her down one day and say, "Mommy, I'm gay" She would never even wish the gay lifestyle on her worst enemy. Gays and lesbians go through too many issues, especially in the black LGBT community. Reagan nearly lost her life because of someone else's beliefs. Reagan decided to find a good church to raise her kids in. Her plan was to go with them and not actually get involved herself.

One Saturday, she was in her driveway washing her car when she noticed a group of people walking down the street going from house to house passing out flyers and appearing quite excited about what they were doing. The kids with them were full of life. Everyone had a lot of joy, Reagan could use some joy at this point. They brought energy to her somewhat quiet neighborhood.

A young couple approached Reagan and introduced themselves as the Pastors David and Crystal of *Christians Are Living Community Ministries*. They gave her a flyer and invited her out to their church service for the upcoming Sunday morning. Reagan became very interested in their church because they were so down to earth, and they were both wearing jeans. They just looked so comfortable. Reagan was not used to this: the Pastors and First Ladies didn't wear jeans to a church function at the churches she was accustomed to. And they certainly didn't introduce themselves on a first-name basis.

Reagan woke up early the next morning. The kids were with Cass for the weekend. I should go check out that church today while the kids are away, she found herself thinking. Reagan would sometimes catch Mr. Fletcher's sermons on TV in hopes of catching a quick glimpse of Brooklyn and Lindan in the audience. She would see Lindan with her grandmother but never Brooklyn. She had heard through the grapevine that, after their break-up, Brooklyn moved away, leaving Lindan with her parents but Reagan didn't know if that was true.

To Reagan's surprise, Mr. Fletcher had started a series of teachings titled "Loving You Where You Are." He also started a movement called NO GUILT, which stood for Never Omit God's Unity In Love Together- an organization to help those living a homosexual lifestyle to understand they still belong to God because love is unity, not division. And he even encouraged the LGBT community to attend his church. Never in a million years would Reagan have thought this the day would come when she walked out of Brooklyn's house. Reagan even heard through some friends that one gay man had decided to live a life of celibacy after becoming a member of Mr. Fletcher's church. With true love ALL things are possible; churches and most Christians need to understand this and stop serving "sinners" with judgment all the time; knowing full well they can't even pick up the first stone, let alone cast it.

Reagan walked into the church and a warm sensation came all over her body. She felt comfortable, like she should be there. She noticed some of the same kids that were running so freely and full of energy around her neighborhood the morning before dancing in front of the praise team. They sang like angels and Reagan could feel the spirit of God all over the building.

Pastor David was introduced when it came to the sermon portion of the service. He came to the stage and began to sing "When The Spirit Of The Lord" and man that church was jumping! Everybody was dancing around the sanctuary singing along with him. "I will dance like David danced." It was amazing. When he began to teach the word he spoke plainly and down to earth. He taught on real life issues, never once using the prehistoric references most preachers used. It was as if he was having a conversation with someone over lunch or while watching a game together. Reagan was shocked at how comfortable he made her feel during the message. And he was comical with some of his references. Surprisingly not once did Reagan look down at her watch. He spoke on how God's desire for you was to live and not die, to have life abundantly. This explained the name of the church, Christians Are "Living;" they sure were full of life here.

Pastor David finished up his sermon and went right into the altar call part of the service. Reagan stood there with her eyes closed and kept feeling an overwhelming tug at her heart to go up there, go to the altar for prayer. The feeling and need for prayer became so overwhelming until finally Reagan walked up to the altar, threw up her hands and began to cry.

Reagan and the kids did join Christians Are Living church and did quite well there. The kids joined just about every ministry the church had to offer the youths. Reagan stayed pretty busy with the kids' extracurricular activities, both with school and church. She even served in a couple of ministries for the church, working her way up to second in command in one of the church's major ministries.

Reagan found staying busy in ministry helpful because it defiantly kept her mind off women. Let's be very clear, though: in the ten years served in ministry and attempting to live a life of celibacy or lesbian free, Reagan still had feelings for women and still found women attractive. That's why she found it hard to believe when people said they were totally free and delivered from homosexuality. Not saying it couldn't happen, but Reagan tried very hard to stay away from women. She thanked God every day for her deliverance because she truly wanted totally deliverance for herself.

Reagan was inspired by the story of Boaz and Ruth. Reagan knew she didn't want another husband, but she studied the book of Ruth and wanted to model her life after Ruth. She felt if she served in ministry along with keeping herself busy raising her kids, God would bless her with deliverance from her sexual desires for women.

Reagan enrolled in a local film school and began working on a digital cinematography degree, a trade she had picked up from church. She worked night shift on her regular job and went to school during the day. Ironically, Reagan met and fell in love with a young lady named Donna. Initially, Reagan beat herself up for her ultimate fall to women. She felt she had let her church, children, family and friends down by going back to the lesbian lifestyle. It took a while before she realized she wasn't a failure because she was happy, and the only way she could ever make others happy was by first finding happiness within her, kinda like the oxygen mask on the plane.

Going to church was a vital part of Reagan's life. She no longer goes because of how Christians can make you feel when what they perceive as sin shows on the outside.

You see, sin is all up and through the church but the problem is most of it is hidden sins. This enables those with hidden sins to sit up in church guilt-free. If the preacher rarely speaks against their issue because it's not an "out in the open" sin, meaning, no one knows but them and God. Therefore, they sit there shouting Amen and clapping their hands as if they are free.

When someone from the LGBT community goes to church, especially when it's someone who's known for their sexual preference or is flamboyant with it, preachers seem to preach hard on sexual sins in their presence.

This does not change who that person is; it actually drives them further from the church.

As for Reagan, she truly misses praise and worship and hearing Pastor David teach the word of God. Not to say preachers shouldn't preach about what they believe as it relates to homosexuality.

Reagan just felt like, when most preachers identify gays or lesbians in their audience they then make a conscious effort to preach against homosexuality, and condemning them to burn in hell. Unfortunately, this tactic only pushes them further away from the church. This very method goes against the teachings in the Bible because the preachers are using the pulpit as a way or excuse to judge others. (*Matthew 7:1-6*)

Reagan's grandmother used to always say, those who are wise are the ones who win the most souls. You have to use wisdom if you want to win others to Christ. Reagan didn't began to fully understand what her grandmother meant by this until she lived her life fully as a lesbian, because that's when she received her worst treatment from "judging" Christians. Most Christians tend to make the mistake of replacing the teaching of loving others with judging others.

Some "church folk" take it way too far. When Reagan fell in love with Don, she was still serving in ministry in the beginning because she was torn and confused on how she should handle it. Reagan and Don would use every tool available to them for communication purposes since they both were so busy with school, work, and church for Reagan.

Reagan also used her personal email account for church business. One day she forgot to log out of her email account on one of the church computers. One of the Elders of the church whom she trusted and worked very closely with used the computer behind her instead of just logging her out of the account and going on about his business.

Violating her privacy, he searched through her personal emails and found some intimate ones between her and Don.

He proceeded to report Reagan to the pastors of the church and she was asked to step down from her church leadership position. Reagan totally agreed with and understood the decision of the church leadership. However, what the Elder did was totally out of order. He had no business going through her personal emails.

But let's look at why he may have done this. It sent the message to Reagan that he simply didn't trust her and was looking for what he found. Yes, his intuitions were right but who gave him the right to judge? So, for Reagan, some "church folk" take it way too far.

That incident left Reagan feeling that certain ones in the church never really believed in her because of her past. If you talked to 100 people from the LGBT community who does not have a church home and asked them that if

129

"church folks" would take their first instinct of judging them, and replace it with loving them, would they go to church more often; the masses would say yes. Christians must develop the mindset to want to see all of God's children *living life abundantly. After all they still belong to God, don't they?*

←CHAPTER NINE→
Python

Donna was going to school to become a music producer. She was a rapper and had a strong desire to get into the music industry. She liked to be called Don and only allowed her mother to call her Donna. She was the total opposite of what Reagan was attracted to. And she had to work extra hard to get Reagan to give her the time of day.

Reagan and Donna had a physiology class together, Reagan noticed this boyish looking girl was always looking and smiling at her in class whenever she looked up. Don was able to get Reagan's phone number because they had to work on a class project together. Don was always texting and calling Reagan long after the project ended, always telling her how much she liked her and wanted to get to know her, even though she had a girlfriend who she lived with.

To this day, Reagan has no idea how she gave in to Don, since they had absolutely nothing in common. They were raised in two totally different parts of the city, Reagan was raised in church, and Don was raised in the streets and even sold drugs. Reagan had a tremendous fear of snakes and Don owned a python. Reagan always went for and was attracted to feminine girls and Don was what was called a Stud. Reagan had never been with a stud as hard as Don before.

Don was mixed race, had tattoos all over her arms and back, used a man's wallet, and wore men's clothing, shoes, and underwear. Don even wore her hair cut like a dude; she walked and talked just like the guys in the hood. This was something new for Reagan - she'd never dated anyone like this before. When they went out to dinner,

Reagan felt uncomfortable at first because she felt as though all eyes were on them because of how Don acted and dressed. She was from the east side of Atlanta and had a very strong street slang.

Things moved very fast with Don. She visited Reagan's house after their first date and never left; she moved her stuff in, including the snake a few days later. There never seemed to be a dull moment in their relationship.

Early one morning just before the end of her shift, Reagan was sitting at her desk and heard a beep on her cell phone. It was a text from Don;

Don:
Thank you ho
for taking this
fucking demon
off my hands!
You home wrecking bitch!

Reagan decided not to reply to the text. Don should have been home and if so, who was texting from her

133

phone? Reagan decided to call her youngest daughter Cassandra who should be up getting ready for school to see If Don was home.

"Hello?" Cassandra answered.

"Hey, is Don at home?" Reagan asked.

"No, ma'am, she hasn't been here since she left to drop you off at work last night." Cassandra said.

"Okay, let me call you back," Reagan said.

She hung up the phone, beads of sweat forming on her forehead. She dialed Don's phone and began having an argument in her mind; *this bitch has my car, living in my house, and has her ex texting me while I'm at work!* She waited for Don to answer the phone.

"Yeah, bitch, dats right. She wit me!" some ghetto female answered.

From time to time whenever Don felt like hanging out all night with friends or exes, she would do so knowing full well Reagan would forgive her. Reagan continued to fight with herself internally over and over about this. She'd never accepted this type of behavior from anyone before and couldn't understand why she was allowing Don to treat her this way. Don was well known in her community because she was mixed race with green eyes. All the ladies wanted her and Reagan loved that she was the one Don said, "I love you bae" to every night, even though the love was false.

After two years they were still together and Don began to show even more of her true colors and the hidden demons she had within. She became super-controlling and mentally abusive. She would tell Reagan she needed to wear heels, dresses, makeup and hair weaves. Don would say, "I need a bad bitch on my arms, you look like a nigga, shawty."

Reagan cried herself to sleep many nights, praying and asking God why; Reagan didn't understand her own actions and wondered why she allowed Don to control her.

135

She couldn't understand how she could agree to have a snake in her house, not to mention every time she went in her woman cave to watch TV, she had to see it slithering in its cage. She was always fearing and never knowing when or if it would get out of its cage. Reagan woke up several times during the night sweating and had multiple nightmares that the snake had gotten in her bed and squeezed the life out of her.

One of the biggest issues, Reagan and Don had been with Reagan's kids. Don absolutely didn't like Reagan's kids and the feeling was mutual because the kids hated Don. And she constantly found reasons to complain about them, especially Cassandra, the baby girl. Cassandra demanded a lot of Reagan's attention and Don didn't like that. Reagan always vowed she would never allow anyone to come between her and the kids. But yet she was doing exactly that.

One day, Don was not in a good mood after getting a very bad review on a song she'd produced for a client. She came home and decided to play the song for Reagan and the kids and wanted their feedback. Little did she know the kids were a lot like Reagan - brutally honest. Needless to say, the kids didn't like the song at all and made it very clear.

"That's a weak beat!" Said Justin. They all began to laugh and make fun of the beat, which infuriated Don. She went to the bedroom and didn't come out for the remainder of the evening, not even for dinner. Reagan put Don's plate on a food tray and took it to the bedroom.

Later that night, after making sure the kids were in bed, Reagan made her way to the bedroom. Don was lying on the bed scrolling through her phone. She had a very unpleasant look on her face and didn't even look up as Reagan maneuvered around the room. The food tray was still on Don's nightstand untouched.

137

"What's wrong with you?" Reagan asked.

Don looked up with a snarled look on her face.

"I'm sick and tired of your bad-ass, disrespectful kids," she snapped.

"What are you talking about?" Reagan asked. "You asked them for their opinion, and you couldn't handle it."

Don stood up and walked towards Reagan.

"Fuck you! Fuck you, and your damn kids!" Don said, exploding.

"Fuck my kids?" Reagan asked.

Reagan never saw it coming but Don hit her dead in the face and knocked her out. When she came to, Don was straddled on top of her with both hands around her neck, choking the life out of her. Reagan remembered what her grandmother always told her. *Sweetheart, if you ever find yourself in any kind of trouble you just call on the name of Jesus and He will answer your prayer.*

Reagan began thinking on Jesus and calling on Jesus and the blood of Jesus, over and over in her head. Don was squeezing tighter and tighter, letting out this awful scream when all of a sudden she let go. By the time Reagan regained her composure and got up off the floor, Don was no longer in the room. Reagan jumped up and immediately searched the house to make sure her kids were still sleeping safely in their beds. She checked the garage to find Don's motorcycle was gone.

Reagan contemplated calling the police to have Don arrested, but decided against it, even though she ended up with a huge knot on her forehead, another broken nose, sore neck, and very bad headache. Reagan knew she couldn't have Don around her kids another day. At this point, all she was concerned with was figuring out the best way to get this lady out of her house and her life.

The next morning, Reagan woke up and Don was in the bed snuggled up beside her. There were a dozen roses on the dresser. Reagan wondered how to get out of bed without waking Don up. She knew she needed some time to herself; she didn't want to talk to Don right now, and give Don the opportunity to work her charm and talk her way out of this.

Reagan needed to get to her mom because her mom would hold her accountable to do what needed to be done. One of the biggest mistake victims of abuse make is not telling someone what you're going through. You must tell that someone in your life who will hold you accountable to do what you don't have the courage or strength to do on your own.

Don moved and changed positions, turning to the other side of bed. Reagan took advantage and immediately got out of bed. She went to the bathroom and burst into tears when she saw her swollen and bruised face, and the red marks around her neck in the mirror. Don choked her so hard it hurt her to swallow her own spit.

Reagan and the kids went to her mom's house for breakfast. Reagan's mom saw right through Don from the start and never liked her for her daughter. She was very upset when she saw Reagan's face and neck. Reagan told the kids she slipped and hit her head; they were young and believed whatever she told them back then. Reagan wasn't too sure Justin bought the story.

"You need to get her out of your house before you end up dead. Once an abuser always an abuser," said her mom.

"I know mama, I know," Reagan replied.

Around mid-morning, Reagan's phone rang, it was Don. Reagan took a deep sigh, regretting the conversation that was about to take place.

"Hello," Reagan answered.

"Hey, do you know what happened to that snake?" Don asked.

"Now you know, I know nothing about that snake," Reagan said sarcastically. "And what do you mean what happened to it?" Reagan asked. "It better not be missing in my house." Reagan stated.

"Naw, it ain't missing, it's dead!" Don said with shock. There was a long pause. "Hello?" Don said.

"Listen Don, It's really clear to me now. I can no longer do this. I need for you to get all of your things and get out of my house. The kids and I will stay with my mom for one week, so by next Saturday, I need you out. I will come back then with the police," Reagan explained.

"Fuck you, I'm not going anywhere!" Don yelled. Fuck, I'm supposed to go Reagan?"

"Don, I have taken pictures of the bruises on my face and neck, and I will go to the police and press charges if I have to, so my advice to you is for you to get out of my house by next Saturday like I've asked you to.

Good bye and I'm hanging up now," said Reagan, and hung up the phone.

Reagan took a deep breath and slowly exhaled. She sat down on a small bench on her mom's porch. Covering her face with her hands, she dropped her head down to her lap, feeling as though someone had taken a weight off her shoulders. Reagan began to think about all of the signs she saw early on in the relationship but ignored simply because she wanted to love and be loved. Reagan knew she had to get herself together before one of the kids came on the porch looking for her. She knew she still belonged to God because He kept on doing great things for her. Once again, God saved her life.

Reagan remembered what Don said about the snake being dead. Could God have taken the life out of that snake at the very moment he sent his angels to stop Don from choking the life out of her? It was too much of a coincidence for Reagan to ignore. The relationship was squeezing the life out of her long before Don actually put her hands around her neck. *Toxic relationships are just like pythons -they will slither around quietly with one goal only, and that is to suck the life right out of its victim.*

←CHAPTER TEN→
My Lady, My Love

Everything about her relationship with Don was proved to be wrong, yet Reagan found it very difficult to get over her. It's true what they say about opposites attracting.

One of the things Reagan missed the most from her relationship with Don was actually living with her significant other. That was the first woman she'd ever lived with. She loved the way Don held her close and tight during the night and constantly told her "I love you Bae." They did share a lot of laughs together; funny thing was it only came when they were alone. Essentially, Don seemed to be a better person one on one, but for some reason around other people, she liked to send the message that she was unhappy.

Reagan wanted a serious relationship so bad until she decided to turn to Internet dating just a few weeks after her break-up with Don, even though she knew deep down this was way too soon. You see, Don tore her self-esteem down so much until she had to find out if other women would find her attractive.

While with Don, Reagan gained forty pounds and by the time she paid the household bills, took care of the kids, and kept Don fitted with the latest Polo and J's, Reagan rarely had any money left over to take care of herself. Don demanded that Reagan cook three meals a day, no matter how tired she was after school and work. The sex was great when they actually had it. Don made a point to deny Reagan of sex, and constantly made references to how good her sex life was with all of her ex-girlfriends. All of these things left Reagan feeling worthless, and unattractive.

146

Reagan began working out, and making smarter eating choices, she lost 40 pounds, got a new hairstyle, and a whole new wardrobe. She created a new profile on a very popular dating web site and waited to see if she would get any hits.

One night, Reagan was away on business and like most nights during that time, she couldn't sleep, tossing and turning all night. She looked over at the clock on the nightstand: it was 02:00 and she was still awake. She grabbed her phone and began scrolling through social media.

Oh wow, look at all the likes I got on the pictures I posted yesterday! I really love my makeover and new look, she thought.

Reagan put her phone down and grabbed her laptop from the other side of the bed, to see if she had any hits on the dating site she created. She had created an awesome profile on the site, answering all of the compatibility questions with honesty. Reagan had the misconception that as long as she was honest and true, she would attract the same. Boy was she wrong. What Reagan didn't realize at the time was when you can't go from one relationship to another still broken and hurt from the past and not give yourself time to heal. What happens is the user and abusers out there smell that weakness on you like a predator can smell blood on its prey.

Almost immediately, Reagan began to receive messages and requests to meet various women on the site. The problem she was having was that most of the women were half her age, either younger or older, BBW, or Studs. She had nothing against any of them; they were just not what she was looking for. Reagan actually liked Studs but feared they would share Don's feelings about her. She had just lived her life in bondage and now wanted a free relationship – 100 percent free - to be whom she truly was within. After ending her last relationship with a dominant

148

Stud and being made to feel ashamed for loving sports, sneakers, and wearing her hair short, Reagan had no desire to go through that type of judgment again.

She never understood why black lesbian women fought so hard for equal rights and went around quoting "only God can judge me," yet are so quick to judge one another as it relates to the Fem vs. Stud stereotype. She truly adored and loved Don in the beginning but Don never gave Reagan a true chance because of how others perceived her as a soft stud or tomboy.

After a month of being on the dating site, Reagan decided to cancel her profile. She wanted to cancel the profile because she felt bad for not having the desire to connect with any of the women who were reaching out to her and never liked wasting anyone's time - especially her own - as she was a true Capricorn.

Reagan had to catch a flight back to Atlanta the next morning, but since she couldn't sleep, she continued to read through the messages she'd received from various women. One notification stood out to her as she combed through the pictures. *I'mJustMe would like to meet you.* Without much enthusiasm as to what to expect, she clicked on the profile of ImJustMe. She was 5'1, very petite, size 3; beautiful brown skin, beautiful smile with nice white teeth; and alluring eyes to die for. She literally took Reagan's breath away!

As Reagan read her profile it was as if she was reading her own. She was a loner, not many friends. She was a breast cancer supporter; they were five years apart in age. She seemed extremely feminine, Christian upbringing, all the things Reagan was looking for, right?

The next day Reagan couldn't get the possibilities of ImJustMe out of her mind so she decided to send her a message once she boarded the plane for Atlanta. Reagan got situated in her seat and began to type:

Good Afternoon,

My name is Reagan I received the notice that you wanted to meet. And I wanted to tell you a little more about myself. I am a business traveler but home in Atlanta every weekend. I truly enjoyed reading your profile, very well put together! I would really like the opportunity to get to know you. Please, let's explore the possibilities! Looking forward to hearing from you.

Take care,

Reagan

Reagan was able to click "send" just before the plane took off and hoped for the best.

Later that night Reagan was sitting in her power recliner having a glass of wine and watching *Scandal*. During one of the commercial breaks, Reagan decided to check her emails in hopes of having a reply from ItsJustMe and, YES, she had responded.

Reagan,

It was nice hearing from you. I must admit I'm a bit jealous

of your business travel. ;) My name is Seven, I'm a very shy

person and keep to myself most of the time. My circle is

very small... I find it to be less drama that way. But I think

I can fit one more. ;) I would absolutely love to get to know

you better. Send me your number and we can chat further.

Looking forward to hearing from you!

Seven

Reagan and Seven started out very promising. Seven always seemed to know exactly what to say to Reagan. If there were one trait Reagan wished she could change about herself after her ordeal with Seven, it would be her soft heart. Seven started the relationship off overwhelming Reagan with things to win her heart, though Reagan didn't realize it at the time.

Seven constantly expressed how she was in mourning over the loss of her son Jeremy due to a car wreck. Ten years ago, Seven's son spent the weekend with a friend and they went out one night. An oncoming driver lost control of the vehicle and hit them. Seven's son was not wearing a seat belt. He did not survive the crash.

Jeremy was Seven's only child; she had conceived using artificial insemination with her previous partner. Seven expressed to Reagan how she wanted to get married and have another child. She really longed to be a mother again. Since her son was taken from her at such a young age.

Reagan took pride in her ability to write poetry and she was effortlessly gifted with words. Whenever Seven would overwhelm her with her problems she would write about it.

One day Seven was having a hard time with her son heavy on her mind so Reagan wrote a little poem to lift her spirits.

His Legacy Lives...

Seven, your son will live forever in you. Through God he will inspire you daily. Never forget his legacy, I won't because I know he is dear to your heart. With your love he is admired for a lifetime.

Reagan fell hard for Seven and made it her mission to make all of her problems go away early on in the relationship. Reagan had always been the type to feel like she had to solve all of her partners' problems. Reagan likely felt this way because no one was ever there to help her in crisis. And being a dominant in the relationship enhanced this trait as well. If Reagan thought Seven wanted or needed anything, she made it happen for her. Through Seven, Reagan's gift of writing was awakened.

←CHAPTER ELEVEN→
The Dark Side of Seven

Reagan absolutely adored Seven and felt like she was the sweetest person she'd ever met. So when she would sit across from her on dinner dates and shed tears about being a mother. And how her mother requested this on her deathbed, Reagan believed her. Seven was everything Reagan wanted in a woman, so much so that Reagan forced herself to ignore the signs that something wasn't quite right with Seven.

Instead she wanted to believe that Seven was this person she allowed her to paint in her mind, the woman her late mother had molded her to be. Seven lost her mother a few years before meeting Reagan and was always speaking of the God-fearing, family-loving mother whom she took after. Reagan fell for this image, daring not to believe the negative signs that were rearing their ugly head.

One thing Reagan noticed early on but ignored because Seven was everything she wanted was Seven's lack of desire to talk on the phone. Most women absolutely loved to talk on the phone, yet this woman never wanted to. Reagan would call instead of text Seven from time to time and the call would go straight to voice mail. On the other hand, Seven would text all day long. Reagan kept reminding herself of all her "girl" talks about men and how you shouldn't trust a man who can't talk on the phone. Shouldn't the same apply with lesbian relationships?

Then it happened. Reagan was sitting in a business meeting when she felt her phone vibrate. She pulled it out of her pocket, excited because she knew this was about the time of morning Seven usually texted her. Sure enough, it was from Seven.

Today 09:45
Seven:
Bestie wants to meet you!!
We are planning a girls
night out next weekend.
Can you come?

Today 10:30
Reagan:
Sure let's discuss.

Now Reagan wasn't too sure how she felt about this because she'd begun noticing how Seven seemed to speak of this "bestie" quite a bit lately as they began to get to know each other better. Seven had her own home, about an hour and a half outside of Atlanta. This house was close to her job, mind you. Yet she stayed at her "bestie's" on her off days. She told Reagan it was to assist her bestie with babysitting. If you seriously date someone for five months, plan to marry them and raise kids. At some point you would spend some of your off days at home and invite them over right?

Seven would always quickly get off the phone with Reagan if Bestie beeped in (on the rare occasions they did talk). At first, Reagan didn't think much of all this; in fact, she felt like it showed just how nurturing Seven was, and would potentially be to her. But after a while, Reagan began to realize this arrangement might not be what was being shared on the surface. As her grandmother Lilly use to say; something in the milk ain't clean.

After observing the situation for a few weeks, Reagan noticed how Seven was the one who was always with Bestie's kids. Seven literally spent her off days taking care of this woman's kids. She was the one who fed, bathed, helped them with homework, took them to football, and cheerleading practices, went on field trips, and other class functions. Even if Bestie went Seven would still go. They were looking more like a couple than Besties.

This bothered Reagan. It made her feel as though Seven had no time for Seven. Seven spent half of her week working long hours and the other half taking care of her Bestie's kids. It only drove the passion deeper into Reagan to marry Seven and make her a mother again.

That next weekend came around pretty quick and, since Reagan traveled for work, she hadn't had time to go shopping for the girls' night out event planned for her to meet Bestie. Reagan woke up early and went to the mall to pick up a few things. She spoke to Seven via text only to find out

Bestie had her running errands for the girls' night event. Seven was so stressed out from going store-to-store buying the alcohol and snacks for the party and for her outfit. She even had to take Bestie's car for a wash. The hardest thing was for Reagan to keep her mouth closed and pretend not to notice because after all, this was her "bestie" so there was no way she'd be taking advantage of Seven.

That night, Reagan arrived at the event and Seven was waiting for her in the hotel lobby. Seven was sitting in a large lounge chair. She looked like a small doll sitting there so beautifully; Reagan was breathless at the sight of her. Reagan walked up to her and gave her a long tight hug.

"Good to see you!" said Reagan.

"Good to see you too, I'm glad you could come," said Seven.

"So…Where's Bestie?" asked Reagan.

"Oh, she's over there checking in," Seven said, pointing at the counter.

Reagan glanced over at the counter and saw a brown-skinned chick with a nicely groomed and naturally curly Afro. She was giving a wad of gum a hard time in her mouth; Reagan could hear the gum popping from where they were sitting.

The chick looked to be a little agitated about something.

"Is everything okay over there?" asked Reagan.

Seven shrugged her shoulders as if to say she didn't know, or maybe she knew better than to say.

Reagan pulled out her phone and began taking pictures of Seven and telling her how beautiful she looked.

"Come on! Let's go!" yelled Bestie, as she handed what looked to be the room key to Seven. This took Reagan by surprise because without any introduction at all, Bestie came out of nowhere, yelling at Seven, demanding she get up and follow her. Seven and Reagan got up and began following Bestie towards the elevator. Inside the elevator, Bestie went on and on about how they were tripping at the front desk. Meanwhile, Seven is fumbling with the elevator controls pushing button after button but the desired floor wouldn't light up. And then without taking a breath Bestie went in on Seven.

"What are you doing? Don't be acting stupid, act like you got some sense," she yelled at Seven yet again.

161

"You know you're supposed to put the room key in the slot in order to get up to the suites. Oh my Gosh!" "Why are you acting retarded?" Bestie was furious.

Meanwhile, Reagan was becoming quite upset, for one thing, because Bestie was acting as if she wasn't even there. Not only had no one introduced them, but also if Bestie was carrying on in this manner in front of a total stranger, how did she treat Seven when they were alone? Everything within Reagan wanted to say something to Bestie for her attitude towards Seven. After all, Seven had spent the day running around town making sure everything was in order for "Bestie's" event. And to hear her yelling at her in this manner was totally not acceptable for Reagan.

Everything finally calmed down once they got settled in the suite and had a couple of drinks. Bestie invited several of her friends over and it was turning out to be a nice little party. Reagan decided to find a nice quiet place to chat with Seven since the majority of their time was usually spent communicating via text. Reagan noticed

Seven was sitting alone on a love seat with her phone in

one hand and a drink in the other. Before she could make it

to Seven she felt her phone vibrate. She pulled her phone

out of her pocket and it was a text from Seven.

Today 9:00
Seven:
*Hey, I think we
should give Bestie
some money to help
her out with this event.
She's been going through
a lot lately. What you think?*

Today 9:03
Reagan:
*Okay, babe whatever
you think. Just let me
know and I'll go the
ATM. I saw one
downstairs.*

Reagan stuck her phone back into her pocket, got a drink and walked over to Seven, grabbed the phone out of her hand and put it on the coffee table in front of them.

"I think I'm a little more interesting than that thing, wanna give me a try?" Reagan asked.

Seven graced her with that beautiful blush of a smile.

"Now that's how I like to see you looking, not all frigid and fragile like you were in the elevator." Reagan said.

It was if someone turned on a switch, because Seven's demeanor immediately changed when Reagan said that. She put a cold, blank look on her face, staring deep and hard at Reagan.

"What are you talking about?" Seven asked.

"In the elevator, sweetie. Why were you allowing her to speak to you that way?" "You seemed so afraid of her and I'm not understanding why." Reagan explained.

"Why are you causing problems?" Seven asked

"Huh?" Reagan said, now very confused.

Here she was trying to show this lady how much she cared for her and didn't want anybody taking advantage of her or mistreating her and all this girl could say is she was causing problems. Not only that asking Reagan to give Bestie money on top of it all.

"Why are you causing drama?" Seven asked again, with the same tone and blank look on her face.

"Sweetheart, the last thing I want concerning you is drama," Reagan responded.

Seven got up, grabbed her phone and walked away. Reagan could see her talking to everybody in the room the rest of the night, except her. In fact, no one seemed to want to talk to Reagan that night. She spent the night enjoying her drinks and music alone, thinking and questioning herself for even being there.

Things changed drastically after meeting Bestie. It seemed as though every other week after meeting her, Seven got mad at Reagan for one reason or another and it required Bestie to fix the situation. Reconciliation usually required Reagan to spend money on a gift.

For example, Seven called Reagan once a week on Saturday mornings at 11:00. This was the only time they talked on the phone. The only other communication they had was via text messages, and a weekly date on Friday nights. They would talk up until Bestie got home from work at which point, Seven had to get off the phone, another sign of something in the milk not being clean that Reagan chose to ignore. There were way too many FLAGS in which Reagan ignored.

Earlier that morning before receiving her call from Seven, Reagan received a call from Don. Reagan stared at her caller ID contemplating whether or not to answer, as she knew this call could only lead to unwanted drama.

"Hello," Reagan answered.

"What's up?" asked Don

"Not much, what's going on?" Reagan asked.

"Can you meet me for lunch today?" Don asked.

"Meet you for lunch? For what?" asked Reagan.

"I need to talk to you about something," Don pleaded.

"You're gonna have to talk to me now, I don't feel comfortable meeting you anywhere!" Reagan expressed.

"What the fuck you mean, you don't feel comfortable?!?" Don exclaimed, now becoming very agitated.

"I don't feel comfortable." Reagan repeated. "After the way you acted during our break-up? The threats you've made against my family and me? No, I don't feel comfortable."

"It's because of your new girlfriend isn't it?" Don asked.

"No, it's my decision," Reagan said.

"Yes it is! I know that bitch won't approve of you meeting me," Don taunted.

"I don't want to meet you, it's my decision," Reagan said.

"We were together two years, and you can't do this one thing for me?" Don asked.

"Listen, it's over. I don't owe you anything, Don," That's final, I'm not meeting you. If you have something to say, then say it now," Reagan affirmed.

"Then fuck you. I promise you I'm going to find that bitch you're seeing and I'm going to fuck her up!" Don yelled.

"Okay, I'm hanging up now, good day to you," said Reagan and hung up the phone. Reagan immediately called her service provider and changed her phone number.

When Reagan spoke to Seven later that morning mainly to give her the new number, she also felt it best to share the conversation she'd had with Don. Reagan wanted to have an open and honest relationship with Seven even though she was seeing signs of something not being quite right with Seven. Reagan thought her good deeds in the relationship would outweigh the bad vibes she was pretending not to see. She felt like Seven had enough good in her to see her genuine loyalty which would in turn make Seven do right by her. Reagan told Seven everything, about her conversation with Don even adding, "I understand if you feel this is not what you want. I know you don't like drama and I can assure you I would not allow Don to hurt you, but, if you feel you need to walk away from this I totally understand."

Talk about an emotional roller coaster because according to Seven, this meant Reagan was throwing in the towel and giving up on them. There was a dead silence on the phone. "I got to take this call. I'll call you later, it's Bestie," Seven announced and abruptly ended the phone call.

This totally confused Reagan. How can she just end the conversation to talk to her bestie? Seven did this quite often and Reagan overlooked it, of course, but for her to do it after Reagan just shared what she'd just gone through really upset Reagan. Reagan felt this was very insensitive on Seven's part. Reagan didn't hear from Seven the rest of the day; she didn't reply to any of her text messages or anything. Reagan didn't know why she was getting the cold shoulder.

That Monday morning, Reagan was sitting at her desk when she received a text message from Seven's bestie.

Today 08:10
Bestie:
*What's going
on with Seven?*

Today 08:21
Reagan:
*Really wished I knew
she won't talk to me...*

Today 08:24
Bestie:
Call me.

Desperately wanting to hear from Seven and how she was doing, Reagan decided to go ahead and call Bestie, since this seemed to be the only way to get to Seven. Even though everything within her told her not to do it, Reagan was a firm believer of don't start none, won't be none. She knew if she started out allowing Bestie to get involved with their affairs, then that's how it would be. Reagan was a very private person and didn't anyone but her taking care of what was hers.

Reagan was right, that phone call proved to be the start of something very much wrong with what Reagan wanted to be so right. Bestie would reach out to Reagan whenever she felt Seven was "unhappy" about something, and request for Reagan to buy perfume, jewelry, clothes, spas and more.

Reagan continued to do so even though she suspected they were returning the gifts for money. She came to this conclusion because there were several gift items Reagan never saw again after she gave them to Seven.

One day Reagan decided to surprise Seven with baby care products for their soon-to-be IVF conceived child. Funny thing, A couple of days later Bestie posted a picture of all the items on social media as if she'd purchased the items for Seven. Reagan was devastated by it yet even after this she continued to hold on to the relationship.

As if that wasn't enough; one of the major signs of any relationship doomed to failure is when one of the parties won't allow you to express your concerns about the relationship. They may feel you are "asking" too many questions, they will usually become easily angered by this. This became evident to Reagan her birthday weekend.

For her birthday Reagan decided she really wanted to spend some quality time with Seven. The kids were with Cass for the weekend so Reagan had the house to herself.

She decided to have a nice romantic meal and a movie at her house for their date that Friday night instead of their usual going out. Seven had never been to Reagan's house before and, of course, Reagan had never been invited to Seven's.

They had been dating a few months by now so Reagan didn't see any harm in having Seven over for some alone time. After all, Reagan had been nothing but a gentle lady with Seven. She'd never made a move in a sexual manner towards her so far; to that point they'd only held hands a few times.

Seven came over to Reagan's house to pick her up for their usual Friday night date but refused to get out of the car and come inside.

"No, I'm not going inside. I'm only here to pick you up," said Seven.

This really threw a monkey wrench in Reagan's plans because not only did she have a surprise dinner waiting inside for Seven, she also had a dozen of roses waiting for her on the coffee table even though it was Reagan's birthday. There were ten red roses for their love and two pink ones to represent her mother's battle with breast cancer two year ago. Reagan wasn't in her life during that time and wanted to make up for it every chance she got.

Reagan was always a very caring and loving person and always made the mistake assuming people would treat her right based on her actions of first doing right by them.

Seven continued to stand her ground with Reagan and refused to get out of the car. Reagan expressed her feelings on how Seven should trust her.

"Haven't I proved myself already?" Reagan pleaded.

"I'm not going in your house!" Seven stated.

Reagan gave up. Pressuring someone to do anything was not her move. "Okay, just go inside and I will sit here in the car," Reagan requested.

"There's something for you on the coffee table, you will see it as soon as you walk in."

"NO!" Seven reasserted.

Without saying a word, Reagan opened the door, got out of the car, went inside and got the roses. She got back into the car with the roses and handed them to Seven.

"This is why I wanted you to go inside, I wanted you to have this," Reagan explained.

Seven started crying at first sight. "But it's your Birthday, Why are you buying roses for me on your birthday?" Seven asked.

"Because honey, birthdays are blessings and I want you to know I'm blessed to have you in my life," Reagan said. "And the two pink ones represent the two years your mom has been gone, and to remind you I'm here. I do love you, Seven.

That being said, I respect your decision so let's go out. I won't pressure you to go inside my house." With Seven breaking down and crying at times like this made Reagan feel like there was some good within her. She felt like if she kept showing Seven how true her heart was she would eventually walk away from her corrupt ways. Reagan believed that even if Seven and her Bestie was actually a couple with the plot of running game on her. She could possibly win Seven from her Bestie by showing her how she is suppose to be treated, giving her the will to walk away from that toxic relationship with Bestie and into the arms of Reagan.

Reagan knew deep down in her heart this was

not the behavior of a person who truly loved her. There is not a woman on this earth in love with a man or woman who would not have gone inside their home after four months of them displaying nothing but trust and respect to them. And even if they were a little skeptical, those roses would've done the trick. But, Reagan continued to choose blindness instead of the facts she was seeing.

Seven began to turn up the heat about the pregnancy and getting the IVF done. She would talk about it constantly and sent Reagan pictures of the donor and all kinds of literature to read on the subject and what to expect. Reagan would send Seven lists of baby names for them to choose from.

If you knew nothing else about Reagan, you would know how protective she was of her girl and how she didn't want anyone else taking care of what was hers. This was clear to everybody. So when she received a text message from Seven thanking her for depositing five thousand dollars into her account for the down payment on the IVF, you could imagine how hurt and upset she was because she knew she didn't make the deposit.

Reagan had already set up a direct deposit into Seven's bank account of seven hundred dollars a month. So the news of someone else depositing an additional five thousand was confusing. Reagan replied to Seven expressing her concerns about the deposits and how she hadn't made a deposit of five thousand in her account. Seven didn't reply.

The next morning Reagan kept watching her phone for a text from Seven. She never did hear from her. Instead, her bestie texted Reagan with an explanation for the mystery deposit.

Today 04:00
Bestie:
I made the deposit.
We talked about this…
You said you would pay
me back when you got
your bonus.

Today 05:45
Reagan:
I said I would pay it,
not pay anyone back.
The $700 a month was to
take care of whatever she
needed until then.

Today 06:00
Bestie:
I need it back asap.
because I used my
house payment money.

Needless to say, Reagan learned a very hard lesson. She paid the five thousand dollars back for the IVF. Even though the screen shot sent to her of the deposit looked bogus.

And for some reason that Reagan still has no idea of, Seven broke up with her that same day. The very day Reagan transferred the money in Seven's account was the last day she laid eyes on her. Reagan came to terms with the fact that she couldn't blame Seven at all, there were too many signs for her to blame anyone but herself.

All in all, they dated for five months but Reagan knew long before then there was a *darker side of Seven.*

←CHAPTER TWELVE→
Leviticus Eighteen
Random Thoughts...

We are all guilty of ignoring the God-given signs that are put before us to avoid false loves. We choose to ignore those signs for various reasons, some because of things we haven't let go from our past, and others could be because of something we are lacking at that moment.

My story is plain; I got married at a young age in order to hide the person I really was deep inside. I lived a life of misery suppressing my feelings because I didn't want to hurt those around me. I didn't want the God who created me to burn me in hell with fire. Being raised in church wasn't a bad thing for me because I feel like I gained a good foundation on life through going to church, and I'm a better person today because of church.

Had it not been for my church upbringing, I

could've really hurt myself, or the some of the people in

my past that hurt and took advantage of me. Instead, I had

the presence of mind to forgive them and keep it moving.

Believe it or not I still have a love for Seven. I feel like I

know exactly what Jesus meant when he said, "Forgive

them Lord for they know not what they do." I still think

about her on certain days of the week and wonder if she's

in her hometown, at work, or at her Bestie's. I once made a

music video for her from a popular song and still think of

her when I hear the song. I do wish her the best.

I don't feel it's God's intent for Christians to judge

and hate non-Christians as they do. In my opinion most

Christians are the biggest hypocrites on this earth. And I

say that because I see Christians whom I like to call

"church folk" judging, disowning, and killing others with

their tongues every day. I call people like that "church

folk" and not Christian because a true Christian wouldn't

behave in that manner. The definition of Christian is Christ-like and, according to the Bible, that's not how Christ behaved. In fact, Christ showed love to all mankind.

I can't explain why I have an attraction for women no more than a heterosexual woman can explain why she has an attraction for men. Why? Because my feelings are just as real and natural to me as her feelings for men are to her. Speaking from a lesbian's prospective, I can honestly tell you this: my desire to love women has nothing to do with my self-esteem, my past history with men, or my inability to get a man. I say that because I'm tired of hearing people say she's too pretty to be a lesbian, or he's too cute to be gay. What does that mean? I feel like people make those comments because they believe if you're homosexual, then something must be mentally or physically wrong with you.

I've been very transparent in this book, the stories you've just read did in fact touch my life in some form or another, and they were all inspired by truth. That being said, yes I was hurt, scarred sexually, abandoned by my father, physically and mentally abused as a child. I believe going through all of these traumatic incidents made me long for attention. And to get that attention I ignored red flags in relationships because I just wanted to feel loved and didn't want to lose the attention I was receiving at that time. Problem was, I always seemed to fall for abusers and users and they were no better than the ones from my childhood.

I remember staying up on the phone all night in the early stage of our relationship listening to one of my ex-girlfriends tell me how she and all of her exes physically fought each other. As if that wasn't enough, I even did a little surfing on the web and found her mug shot for domestic violence. What I should have done was cut the relationship off before it even started. Instead, I walked right into the relationship with my eyes wide shut.

I actually thought my good would outweigh her bad. I was going to church faithfully when I met her so I thought for sure she would respect the fact that I was a "church girl" and not put her hands on me, or verbally abuse me. I quickly learned I was wrong, but I wanted to be in a lesbian relationship so bad I stayed and put up with her for years. I loved her despite her abuse and, I accepted the fact that she didn't really love me in return.

Parents with kids that are struggling with homosexuality please listen to them it's very important to keep that line of communication open. Don't push them away, there are "gay houses" out there that will take your youth in and some of them don't have their best interest at heart.

Young men and women are being molested out there by older men and women who feel as though these kids owe them. The kids put up with this behavior because they feel like they have nowhere else to turn.

185

I've met teenagers who were put out on the street by their blood and these houses gives them a since of belonging.

When a person truly loves you they will put their time, money, and heart where their love is. They will spend time with you, meaning, you will never have to beg them for their time. When you start wondering if someone loves you, why haven't they called me today, why are they cool with "getting to know me" via text, save your time wondering because they do not love you. In fact, they have no true interest in you whatsoever.

You will not go lacking while someone who truly loves you is in your life. They won't have you spending your all on them and not taking care of yourself. They will recognize your needs, desires, pain, and do something about it. They will speak life into you and not death. They will build you up with their words and never tear you down.

To this day I believe my one true love was with a young lady who was raised in the church just as I was. We were forced to end our relationship because her dad is the head pastor of the church. Yes, she was a PK (preacher's kid). Even though we were in our mid-twenties when we met, her dad was still in control of her life. She didn't want to live this lifestyle out in the open, and I totally respected that. You see, I loved her enough to let her go. In other words, I walked out of her life because of my love for her.

I knew how much her father loved her and how important family was to her; I never wanted her to choose between the two of us. I totally understood his stance and how passionate he was about what God wanted for his daughter. I often wonder how she turned out, but when I made the decision to walk away; I did just that.

To the young lady and her bestie, you two took advantage of me. And you are no different from the man that molested me as a child. You saw my heart, and you took it for all you could. I have prayed for you every day since the night you got out of my car, and I will continue to do so. The day you walked out of my life you said that I needed to be taught a lesson. Because you felt like I was "playing you." Now ain't that funny?

The reality of it all is this: you never had any intentions on building a family with me. You never had any intentions of having a relationship with me. You fabricated a reason to walk away and that's fine. My guess is you are a straight girl with a birdbrain, chasing bread, so congratulations. But let me tell you this, my heart is much more valuable than what you feel you walked away with.

I pray for you, because I feel sorry for you. You are abused and don't even know it. I say thank you for teaching me such a valuable life lesson. I learned the hard way that for five months, you were my lady, my love; while I took you for something real; you took me for just a job.

I feel like, I still belong to God. He continues to bless me. I love Jesus so much. I guess that's why it hurts me so much for people to judge me and question my heart towards God.

I believe in my heart that if someone put a gun to my head and say denounce Christ right now or I will kill you. I will stand there flat-footed and look them dead in their eyeballs and say then kill me. You see, only God can judge me. I have No guilt, and I'm free because I know that he knows my heart.

He gave me the NO GUILT phrase: Never Omit God's Unity In Love Together; I want people to know that you can't have unity without love; they work together. And if we can learn to operate in unity and love with one another, how many lives will we touch? How many suicides will we prevent when more people are living guilt free?

The book of Leviticus, chapter 18, speaks on several sexual sins, yet most people only focus on the 22nd verse where if says; *do not have sexual relations with a man as one does with a woman.*

There are 23 total verses on sexual sins. John 8:7 reads: *He, who is without sin, cast the first stone.* This scripture clearly shows how Jesus offered love and not judgment.

I'm not sure what God's plans are for me, in terms of a relationship. Or living a life of celibacy. Right now I have my oxygen mask on, and I'm saving me. I've been single for over a year now.

I'm now a published Author, songwriter, and poet. For the first time in my life I love Harnetha Shantrā and I refuse to allow anyone else to take from me.

I now know my worth and if the next person can't see it soon enough then they are not the one for me. We shouldn't waste time with confused individuals with snake like mentalities. Always remember the signs are there we just have to open our eyes.

←CHAPTER THIRTEEN→
Poems for My Lady

In the five months Reagan got to know Seven, the gift of writing was re-birthed in her. Hopefully, you can enter Reagan's heart by reading her favorite seven poems written for the person who she thought would be her lady;

A Poem for Seven...

I know there's more to you than I can see.
I thank God for the gift he has placed in me.
You're like a precious gem buried in the ground.
With his help your worth will be revealed.
And this is why I stay around.
I love every part of you, things known and unknown.
I want to be there for you, to fight off demons until they're gone.
I will give you a gift, the gift of life.
My desire is to make you a mother, as well as my wife.
In return, I ask for your heart.
And I promise our love will never grow apart.

Hello my lady my love...

Praying for you.
I'm praying for your strength in the Lord and your trust in
him.
I'm praying he will put your heart in his hands and release
his healing power. He is your comforter; find peace in him.
Forever my lady I will love you.

You are to me...

Seven, you are my lady my love my wife.
I want to be with you for the rest of your life.
You are my inspiration; you've brought the gift of poetry to
live in me.
You have opened my blind eyes on love and true love I
now see.
You bring out the best in me because you don't settle for
less.
You once told me; "I'm a lady". And yes you are... the best
You are so beautiful both inside and out.
You love me, you've fallen for me and now I have no
doubt.
You have shown me nothing but kindness right from the
start.
You are protected, I love you lady, I will catch you, guard
you, even your heart.
You're just too good to be true.
I will never take my love from you.

If I were your girlfriend...

I wouldn't want a day to go by without hearing your sweet voice.
I would provide for you, treat you to the things of your choice.
You would always feel my presence whether I'm here or away. Chest to chest with you; heartbeat to heartbeat we would dance to our beat every day.
I would want you to tell me your deepest fears. And I vow to protect you from harm's way. I will be the one to wipe your tears away.
I would build you up, and never tear you down. My intent and purpose is to make you smile, never want to see you frown.
My goal will be to inspire you to live life to the fullest. Never leaving your side, proving to you I'm the realist.
I will make; my lady, my girlfriend, my girlfriend, my lover, my lover, my wife, and my wife, my baby mother.
If I were your girlfriend... Our baby would become a reality.
And all I want in return is for you to truly love me.

I went to church today...

I went to church today to hear a word from the Lord.
While there I was blessed with a vision of us on one accord.
We were together you, our child, and me. Putting God first your arms lifted up as tears flowed down your face.
I held our child, watching her mother for I knew you were grateful to God for this bundle of joy we had only by his grace.
It's your time my dear, God wants you happy. We have to keep him in control.
Together let's put God first giving him our spirit, mind, heart, and soul.
He spoke to me today; he said you've both gone through the storm for this reason.
Together I will bless you both, happiness and love will be in your home this season.
Put your past behind you for I've already delivered you from it.
Now walk in your blessings as a family. Show the world my love is for all and never quit.

Relax lady and let me be your rock!

Relax babe and let me be your comforter.
I know it's hard for you because you've heard it before.
I promise to show you that I will be the one to do you right
this time.
You're my lady and I love you so much. I look forward to
our Friday's to see the city or just wine and dine.
Don't give up on me darling. Sometimes I feel you
wondering did I choose the right one.
Time will prove you've made the perfect choice. I'm here to
build you, love only you, and to have the strongest bond.
I'm here forever to hold you up. You won't have to survive
another obstacle alone. You can put your mind on
autopilot.
Knowing Reagan is here and she got it.
Whatever decision we have to make about the baby we will
make.
I got you ma, I will do everything in my power; whatever it
takes.

Good morning sweet babe my love,

Keep your eyes on the prize and remember it's your time. You brought me back to life. My four-year relationship with my ex squeezed the life right out of me. From the first time I heard your voice until the first time I saw your beautiful face. I've been alive and true to my real self inside and out. Please don't ever doubt, my love for you, it's true. I will never leave turn back or forsake you. I'm a loner and yes forever I'd rather be alone with you. I want to do you right everyday. You will never have to secretly wonder; "Do she still love me?" My actions will show you I do. Sweet babe I thank you for the life you've given me. The inspirations I now have,
I don't want you to worry about a thing. I will repay you with the gift of life a child to call our own, bundle of joy, full of life to bring you happiness forever.

I love you so much ma.

See you soon!

Reagan started writing poems when she was in middle school, but stopped writing them after she married Cass. The passion to write died inside her until what she thought was true love with Seven sparked the gift again. The love she felt for Seven made her feel alive again, it was deep, and she constantly felt compelled to write about it. Even though her love with Brooklyn was the more real love she didn't write until she had the false love with Seven. Funny, how one can have eyes but still can't see;

False Love Always Gives Sight.

FALSE LOVE ALWAYS GIVES SIGHT

F.L.A.G.S.

By

Harnetha Shantrā

Published By
Visions In Motion Productions
ISBN-13: 978-0692661956
ISBN-10: 0692661956

Website: www.harnethashantra.com
Email: harnethashantrā@gmail.com

harnethashantra

Instagram
YouTube
Facebook
Twitter

FALSE LOVE ALWAYS GIVES SIGHT

www.ingramcontent.com/pod-product-compliance
Lightning Source LLC
Chambersburg PA
CBHW031532040426
42445CB00010B/503